The Working Cook

The Working Cook

FAST AND FRESH MEALS FOR BUSY PEOPLE

BY TARA DUGGAN

FOOD COLUMNIST FOR
THE SAN FRANCISCO CHRONICLE

The San Francisco Chronicle Press

Editor: Narda Zacchino

Designer: Dorothy A. Yule

Copy Editors: Sharron Wood,
Jennifer Thelen

Photographer: Craig Lee

Photo Editor: Kathleen Hennessy

Food Stylist: Jen Straus

Business Director: Dickson Louie

Marketing Director: Jennifer Asche

The San Francisco Chronicle

Publisher: Frank Vega

Editor: Phil Bronstein

*Facing the title page: Fish in Spicy
Saffron Broth with Couscous (recipe
on page 105)*

The San Francisco Chronicle Press

901 Mission Street, San Francisco, CA 94103
www.sfchroniclepress.com

ISBN-13: 978-0-9760880-7-3
ISBN-10: 0-9760880-7-X
Library of Congress Control Number: 2005937201

Printed and bound in China

Distributed by Sterling Publishing Co., Inc.

To my working cook family,
Eric, Dahlia & Elsie

Contents

Foreword

The Bay Area is a special place for food lovers, with great raw ingredients, some of the world's best wines right outside our back door, and some of the finest and most diverse restaurants in the United States. It's a food paradise.

Yet, even those of us who live here are challenged by the task of making dinner every night. It seems almost embarrassing to be surrounded by all this bounty and to be strapped for what to cook.

That's what inspired *The San Francisco Chronicle* to create "The Working Cook," which Tara Duggan has written since 1999. The column has become one of the most popular features in the Food section. It is designed to help time-pressed cooks ferret out local ingredients and seasonings, then use them to create nourishing, delicious meals in minutes.

Tara is uniquely qualified for this task. A graduate of the California Culinary Academy, she loves to cook so much that she even catered her own wedding. Tara came from a military family and has lived all over the United States, Italy and Germany. She's traveled to many countries and has developed a particular love for the cuisine of Mexico. She's passionate about quality ingredients and good food, but as a young working mother she understands the need to get dinner on the table quickly.

Tara rises to the challenge with more than one hundred recipes for imaginative dishes like quesadillas with queso fresco and poblano chiles, linguine with vermouth and orange-scented shrimp, maple-glazed pork chops with smashed yams, and Thai red curry with tofu and spinach. These streamlined recipes reflect our ever-increasing craving for exciting global flavors, and they can be on the table in around thirty minutes. Each recipe also has been analyzed for nutritional content.

In the course of producing the column, Tara has developed hundreds of recipes, but for this book she has selected the ones that give the time-starved cook the maximum amount of return for the least amount of effort.

All these recipes passed muster with the sixteen staff members of the Food and Wine sections, which won a James Beard award as being the best in the country. Not only do staff members represent some of the most discriminating palates in the United States, they have a deep understanding of many cultures; within the department, various members speak Thai, German, Italian, French, Spanish, Japanese and three dialects of Chinese.

Tara went one step further in completing *The Working Cook Cookbook* by having home cooks test the dishes. The recipes are now ready for you to enjoy.

Miriam Morgan
Food Editor
The San Francisco Chronicle

> "These streamlined recipes reflect our craving for exciting global flavors, and they can be on the table in around thirty minutes."

Opposite, Tara Duggan in The San Francisco Chronicle *Food Department test kitchen*

Introduction

My grandmother Dorothy once shared with me the advice she used to give her home economics students in the 1950s: when you serve your husband a frozen dinner, fry up some onions right before he comes home so that the house smells like you have been cooking all day.

Most men no longer expect their wives to make them a home-cooked meal every night, but the desire for tantalizing aromas coming from the kitchen remains. The popularity of food programs on TV, culinary magazines, and showcase kitchens reveals a longing for homemade food, even though the reality for many Americans is that dinner regularly comes out of the freezer or a takeout container.

Not only do home-cooked meals taste good, but they are also better for you than restaurant food because they give you more control over portion sizes and ingredients. The challenge for most people, however, is finding enough time in the day to shop for ingredients, prepare and cook them, and then clean up afterward.

This book is designed to help all of us with busy lives satisfy the yearning for home-cooked food. Most of the recipes take thirty minutes or less to prepare, and none requires shopping for a long list of hard-to-find ingredients. They are all easy to make and full of fresh vegetables and grains. Most recipes will be all you need for a full dinner; others you might want to serve with a green salad or a simple pot of rice to make a complete meal.

The recipes come from "The Working Cook," a twice-monthly column I have written for *The San Francisco Chronicle* since 1999. With the help of friends and colleagues, I have retested and revised each one for this book to make sure it is as easy, wholesome, and delicious as possible.

The column has evolved along with changes in my life. When I first started writing it, I had recently graduated from culinary school and was eager to exercise my flashy new skills. Like many of my culinary school colleagues, I was passionate about food and happy to spend a leisurely weekend cooking a complex meal. I soon realized, however, that the average working cook does not have this luxury.

For example, there was the reader who called with a cooking question while trying to get ready for a family camping trip. The entire time we spoke, one of her children was crying in the background. She liked "The Working Cook" recipes, but could they be easier? And, by the way, she knew this great recipe for grilled frozen tater tots.

Three years ago, when I gave birth to my first child, I suddenly could relate. My daughter needed snacks and diaper changes, naps and walks. She is an easygoing child, but spending an entire Saturday in the kitchen is out of the question. Often, when I come home from work and see her pink cheeks and hear her little giggle, I don't feel much like cooking at all.

I still want to make fresh food for my family—it is satisfying for all of us—but now it must be easy to shop for and require a minimum of time to prepare. This book is for all cooks who share this goal.

— *Tara Duggan*

Home-cooked meals made with fresh ingredients don't have to be time-consuming.

Fundamentals

This chapter will help get working cooks off to the right start. It explains how to stock your kitchen with food staples and tools that will make life much easier when you find yourself in a hurry to make dinner after a crazy day at work. It also covers cooking techniques so that you won't be intimidated the first time you try to pan-sear a steak, steam a piece of fish or whip up a golden-brown frittata.

Here is what you can expect to find when you begin cooking from this book:

COOKING TIME

The time estimate listed at the beginning of each recipe refers to the total amount of time you might expect to spend making the dish, from peeling and chopping the ingredients to putting the dish on the table. A recipe might take a bit longer the first time you make it, however, as you become familiar with the method.

Grilling recipes will take longer to prepare if you have a charcoal grill, which requires extra time to set up. Each recipe offers alternatives for using the broiler or a grill pan if you're in a rush. And if you love to grill, think about investing in a gas grill: all you do is flip a switch and you're ready to cook in fifteen minutes.

ONE STEP AT A TIME

To make your cooking experience more pleasant, take a minute to read the recipe through and gather all the ingredients and pans you will need before starting. To finish the recipe within the time estimate given, most recipes require starting one task—such as boiling water for pasta, preheating the oven, or marinating chicken—before you proceed with the recipe.

SHOPPING

Experimenting with ingredients from other cultures opens new worlds of flavor, and the recipes in this book emphasize the many exciting ethnic foods now readily available in this country. Most of the ingredients in these recipes should be available at a well-stocked supermarket. I offer substitutes for some of the more unusual ingredients when possible, in case your local store doesn't carry them.

Once you get hooked on a particular type of cuisine, you may find yourself seeking out Latin American, Asian, Middle Eastern, or Italian grocers to stock up on ingredients and to get the best deals on pantry items such as soy sauce, olive oil, vinegar, and spices.

In the meantime, stocking your pantry with a small number of basic ingredients will allow you to make all of the recipes in this book with a minimum of last-minute shopping fuss. See page 16 for a list of suggested pantry ingredients, and the glossary on page 167 for detailed descriptions of some of them.

NUTRITION

Unlike most cookbooks, this book has the added value of including a nutritional analysis for each recipe. I used the National Restaurant Association's Nutrition Recipe Analysis software program, also used by *The San Francisco Chronicle* Food section. (Please see Nutritional Analysis on page 14.)

Though I don't consider this book to

Facing page: Quesadillas with Poblanos, Corn & Pepitas (recipe on page 84)

Nutritional Analysis

◆ The nutritional analysis that follows each recipe does not include optional ingredients.

◆ Garnishes and suggested accompaniments are not included unless specific quantities are given.

◆ When there is a range of servings, the larger number of servings is used.

◆ When there is a range in the amount of an ingredient, the smaller amount is used.

◆ When a recipe lists a choice of ingredients (such as bok choy or napa cabbage), the first is used.

◆ Oil used in frying is not included.

◆ Salt is included in the analysis only when a recipe calls for a specific amount. Salt added to cooking water is not included.

◆ Because of variations in ingredients, all values are approximations.

be about spa cuisine, the recipes are full of grains, fresh vegetables, and fruit, with emphasis on heart-healthy fats from vegetable oils and fish. I've worked on each recipe to make it as low in animal fat, calories, and sodium as possible while still preserving its flavor and character. See pages 170 and 171 for the light and low cholesterol recipe indexes.

A handful of recipes, especially those containing sausage or red meat, have higher sodium, fat, and cholesterol levels than the others. If you or your family members have specific health concerns, I suggest you save these dishes for special occasions or avoid them altogether. You may also choose to substitute olive oil for a pat of butter, or tofu for chicken in a soup or curry, for example.

A lot of salt is used in processing foods such as canned beans and tomatoes. If you're trying to cut down on salt, stock up on lower-sodium products, available in health food stores and many supermarkets. In some recipes with a particularly high sodium count, I sometimes call for products such as reduced-sodium soy sauce.

EQUIPMENT

You won't need specialty equipment to make the recipes in this book, but you may find that a few gadgets offer an advantage when you need to save time. See page 18 for some suggestions on how to best outfit your kitchen with basic pots, pans, and utensils, as well as the accessories that will make life in the kitchen easier.

COOKING SKILL

The recipes in this book should be easy enough for most beginners but still compelling and fun for more advanced cooks. Look to the tips and chapter introductions for information on some of the techniques used in these recipes, such as the best way to cube a mango, cook pasta, or make a vinaigrette.

QUICK-COOKING TECHNIQUES

Understanding a bit of the science behind cooking will help you make smart choices about how to quickly cook different types of ingredients to get the results that you want. Generally, culinary experts divide techniques into dry-heat and moist-heat cooking methods. Dry-heat methods use either radiant heat or hot fat to cook foods quickly and to create a crisp texture. Moist-heat cooking methods involve cooking with steam or hot liquid. The following are the main quick-cooking techniques used in this book.

DRY-HEAT COOKING METHODS
BROILING AND GRILLING

Broiling and grilling utilize high, indirect heat to create a crisp, golden crust and smoky flavor. Usually only a very small amount of fat is used to coat the grill or pan, which means that food can dry out easily, so it's important not to overcook it. It also helps to marinate the food before cooking it and to serve it with moist accompaniments like sauces, salsas, and salads. When broiling, place the pan about four inches from the heating element.

PAN-FRYING

Unlike deep-frying, which involves immersing foods completely in hot fat, pan-frying requires filling a pan with only one to two inches of oil, so that it reaches halfway up the food you are

Searing Meat or Fish

To create a crispy, golden-brown crust on a steak, chicken breast, or fish fillet, it is important to use a very hot pan; otherwise, the food will stick to the cold metal, as well as absorb more of the fat. If you place cooking oil in a cold pan, it will reach its smoking point before the pan has had time to heat up properly, so heat the pan before adding the oil.

Regular frying pans, without a nonstick coating, are best for searing. Nonstick pans can give off potentially dangerous fumes when they are left on high heat without anything in the pan.

For the best results when searing, follow these steps:

◆ Season the piece of meat or fish well on both sides with salt and pepper.

◆ Heat a heavy pan over medium-high heat until quite hot. This may take a few minutes. To test the pan, place your hand a few inches above it; you should feel the heat rising from the pan.

◆ Add enough oil to coat the entire bottom of the pan, and heat it until it is shimmering but not smoking.

◆ Carefully add the meat or fish. The oil should sizzle. When searing more than one item at a time, don't crowd the pan, or the temperature will drop too much and you might end up steaming the food rather than browning it.

◆ Let the meat brown undisturbed for a few minutes until it gets crusty and golden brown. Flip and repeat on the other side.

Basil

Fresh Herbs

Though fresh herbs don't count as a pantry item because they are perishable, they are wonderful to have on hand. Simple, quick-cooking recipes really benefit from their lively flavor. When you're not using a lot of ingredients, or you don't have time to slowly simmer a sauce to build its flavor, adding fresh herbs can really add zest to a dish.

Unfortunately, it can get expensive to buy fresh herbs, especially when you end up using only half of them and throwing the rest away. Heartier herbs such as bay leaves, oregano, rosemary, and thyme retain much of their flavor when dried. Simply use about a third of the quantity suggested for fresh herbs. Delicate herbs such as parsley, basil, sage, and cilantro, however, are much better fresh. Growing some of your favorite herbs in a window box or a sunny spot in your kitchen is a great way to reduce waste and save some money, and most herbs don't require a green thumb to cultivate.

cooking. You fry the food first on one side, and then flip it over to finish cooking. This method is easier for cooking small amounts of food and makes less of a mess than deep frying.

ROASTING

This method uses high oven heat (375°F or higher) to cook large but tender pieces of meat such as pork chops and thick steaks and hearty vegetables such as portobello mushrooms and sweet potatoes. Roasting creates some browning on the outside but allows food to remain moist on the inside.

SAUTEING

This means to cook cut-up food in butter or oil over medium to medium-high heat with frequent stirring until it becomes slightly browned. Sautéing is a fundamental technique used in many of the recipes in this book. For example, to make a tomato sauce, you start with a hot pan, then add oil, then chopped aromatic vegetables such as onions, garlic, and herbs. These ingredients are sautéed until tender, at which point you are ready to add the tomatoes and liquid.

SEARING AND PAN-ROASTING

Searing involves cooking an ingredient over high heat until it browns as it makes contact with the hot pan and oil. Some thin meat and fish fillets will be cooked through after searing, but thicker cuts such as chicken breasts benefit from first being seared in the pan and then finished in a hot oven, a technique that is called pan-roasting.

STIR-FRYING

This method is similar to sautéing, but it calls for higher heat and almost constant stirring and tossing. Stir-frying is best done in a wok because the wok's

rounded bottom facilitates tossing and provides a large surface area. Many stir-fry recipes call for cooking the individual ingredients one at a time so that they are able to maintain contact with the bottom of the pan at all times without crowding.

MOIST-HEAT COOKING METHODS
BOILING

This simply means to immerse foods completely in boiling liquid over high heat. The less time vegetables spend in boiling water, the fewer nutrients and the less flavor and color they will lose, so start with a large pot of water at a rolling boil, which will return to a boil more quickly after the cold ingredients are added. Adding plenty of salt to the water also helps maintain a high heat, because salted water boils at a higher temperature than unsalted water.

SIMMERING

This method, often used in making sauces and soups, is similar to boiling but is done at a lower heat level. A simmering liquid should bubble gently.

STEAMING

Steaming involves cooking food over a small amount of boiling liquid. It can be done with a steamer or in a microwave, as long as the food is covered tightly. Steaming retains more nutrients than boiling and is great for tender vegetables like green beans and for some fish. The moist heat helps prevent the fish from drying out.

PANTRY STAPLES

Keeping the following basics stocked in your pantry and refrigerator will help you prepare fresh meals quickly. Some of these items are described further in the glossary, page 166.

Aromatics such as onions and garlic should be stored in a cool, dark place and replenished often. Ginger should be wrapped and stored in the refrigerator.

After opening, ground spices and dried herbs are intended to last one year, whole spices much longer, so it's a good idea to buy small portions, if possible, and label your herbs and spices with the date you purchased them. If you store your spices tightly wrapped in a dark, cool cupboard, however—not in a rack on top of the stove—they often last longer. Just toss them out when they are no longer fragrant.

Nuts go rancid easily, so don't buy too many of them in advance. If you have leftovers, wrap them in a freezer-safe resealable plastic bag and freeze for use later in salads and pastas.

AROMATICS
garlic
ginger
onions (yellow or white and red)
shallots

CONDIMENTS AND SAUCES
Asian fish sauce
chile-garlic sauce
hot sauce, such as Tabasco
oyster sauce
soy sauce
vinegars (balsamic, rice, champagne, white wine, red wine, sherry, and fruit-flavored)

DRIED HERBS AND SPICES
bay leaves
cayenne pepper
ground coriander
ground cumin
curry powder

oregano leaves
whole black peppercorns
red pepper flakes or dried chile flakes
rosemary leaves
saffron
salt
thyme leaves

FATS
unsalted butter
canola or other vegetable oil
olive oil
Asian or toasted sesame oil

GRAINS
instant couscous
pasta (such as orzo, penne rigate, rigatoni, spaghetti)
rice (short- or medium-grain and long-grain)
rice stick noodles

LEGUMES
beans (canned, including refried, black, pinto, and white)
chickpeas (canned)
lentils (dried green)

NUTS AND SEEDS
almonds, slivered or sliced
pecans
pepitas (shelled green pumpkin seeds)
pine nuts
sesame seeds
walnuts

SPIRITS
brandy or Cognac
rice wine
dry sherry
dry vermouth
dry red and white wine

MISCELLANEOUS
anchovies
bread crumbs
capers
low-sodium chicken broth

Bay leaf

Saffron

Garlic

Olive oil

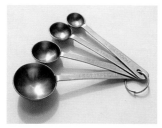

Measuring spoons

Measuring cups

Stainless steel mixing bowls

Flexible spatulas

chipotle peppers in adobo sauce
coconut milk
all-purpose flour
sugar
whole and chopped canned tomatoes
tuna, packed in olive oil

EQUIPMENT FOR THE WORKING COOK

While helping to run and organize the test kitchen in *The San Francisco Chronicle's* Food department, I have learned a lot about the advantages of various appliances and pans. The most important discovery I have made is that having a small collection of well-made tools is worth more than a kitchen full of gadgets.

The following checklist includes all the tools necessary to outfit a basic kitchen and to prepare the recipes in this book. The second list, Extras, contains additional items that aren't strictly necessary but can save you time in the kitchen. Consider putting them on your birthday wish list.

It can be more economical to buy pots and pans in a set rather than purchasing individual pieces, but I don't necessarily recommend this. Most manufacturers do a great job with some items in a set but not so great a job with others. In addition, sets don't always include pots and pans in the sizes you'll use most often.

Similarly, if you're just beginning to acquire quality knives, you don't need to buy an entire set. Start with an eight-inch chef's knife (referring to the length of the blade itself), the knife you will use day after day. Knives with high-carbon steel blades and a full tang, mean-

ing the metal from the blade runs the full length of the handle, are best.

If you can't have everything on this list, start with a couple of solidly crafted pans and knives. They will not only perform beautifully, but they can last for decades if you take good care of them.

BASICS
POTS & PANS

Pots and pans are measured across the top, inside the rim.

Saucepans, small, 1- to 2-quart, for boiling small items such as frozen peas, or making a sauce; medium, 4-quart, preferably with steamer insert

Sauté pan, 3-quart; in this book refers to a pan with straight sides and a lid, used for simmering pasta sauces as well as sautéing and frying

Frying pan or skillet, 10-inch; in this book refers to a pan with sloped sides, which makes flipping fried foods easier; look for a heavy pan with a thick bottom

Frying pan, 10-inch nonstick, good for cooking eggs and delicate fish; again, look for a heavy pan with a thick bottom

Stockpot or pasta pot, preferably with a steamer insert

Cookie sheets, 2 to 3 insulated; great for roasting vegetables and broiling meats as well as baking; heavy-duty pans help prevent burning and are less likely to warp

Baking pan, 13- by 9-inch; heat-proof glass or ceramic is great for roasting meats as well as baking brownies or casseroles

UTENSILS

Knife set, 8-inch chef's, 4-inch paring, serrated knives, and honing steel; you'll also need a knife block or magnet to keep knife edges sharp and protected

Cutting boards, 2 to 3 in various sizes

Mixing bowls, set of nesting stainless steel

Colanders, 1 to 2 large

Fine-mesh strainer

Spoons, assortment of wooden spoons, a slotted spoon, and ladle

Whisk

Slotted spatula, good for removing items from oil

Solid spatulas, including at least one wooden or plastic spatula, which won't harm nonstick surfaces

Flexible spatula, for scraping out bowls

Tongs, 1 to 2 sturdy pairs with a locking device, for grilling and pan-frying

Vegetable peeler

Box grater

Liquid measuring cup set, including 1-cup, 2-cup, and 4-cup measures

Dry measuring cups, stainless steel

Measuring spoons, narrow ones will fit into spice jars

Pepper mill, look for one that grinds very finely

Kitchen timer

EXTRAS

I use most of these items frequently, but whether or not you need them will depend on what foods you most like to cook.

Citrus press or reamer; alternatively, use a pair of tongs to squeeze out the juice

Food processor, necessary for several recipes in this book, such as the Penne with Roasted Eggplant & Pesto, page 69

Nonstick grill pan, a great alternative to setting up the grill

Immersion blender, makes it super-easy to puree soup without removing it from the pot

Instant-read thermometer, easier to read than dial thermometers when testing the doneness of meat

Mandoline, for cutting vegetables into ultra-thin, uniform slices and julienne; the inexpensive plastic versions from Japan are fine—just watch your fingers

Microplane fine grater, perfect for grating fresh ginger, citrus zest, and nutmeg

Oven thermometer, to make sure your oven is calibrated correctly

Rice cooker, makes quick work of cooking rice

Salad spinner, dressing clings better to dry lettuce

Wok, cold-rolled steel woks conduct heat better than nonstick versions, but unlike nonstick woks, they have to be seasoned; follow manufacturer's directions

Instant-read thermometer

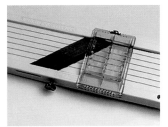

Mandoline

Microplane grater

Rice cooker

Eggs for Dinner

When I think I don't have anything in my kitchen to cook, I usually can find at least a few eggs. Excavating further into the dark corners of the fridge and finding a half-empty can of beans, slightly stale tortillas, and a hunk of cheese, I soon discover that I can concoct a slap-dash version of huevos rancheros, delicious not only for breakfast but also satisfying served as dinner.

Another classic Mexican breakfast dish, chilaquiles, is also an easy way to turn leftovers into dinner. Sautéed in a pan or layered in a casserole, the dish uses up whatever salsa, cheese, tortillas, and eggs you happen to have handy.

The Italian equivalent is a pasta frittata, made from yesterday's cooked pasta bound together with eggs. And because frittatas—open-faced omelets that are partially cooked in the oven—taste fine at room temperature, they are perfect packed in a weekday lunch or served at a picnic. If you don't have an ovenproof nonstick frying pan, use a nonstick frying pan and slide the frittata into an ovenproof pan to finish it in the oven.

Hangtown Fry (recipe on page 23)

21

20 minutes

Serves 4

- ¾ cup grated fontina cheese
- 2 ripe Roma tomatoes, sliced into thin rounds
- 4 to 6 slices prosciutto (about 4 ounces), cut into bite-size pieces
- 10 large eggs

  Freshly ground pepper to taste
- 2 tablespoons olive oil

Frittata with Prosciutto & Tomatoes

This gorgeous combination of fluffy eggs, salty prosciutto, ripe tomatoes, and creamy fontina cheese smells like heaven as it comes out of the oven. Looking something like a pizza, it makes a nice addition to a brunch party. Serve with country bread and a salad.

Preheat the broiler while you prepare the cheese, tomatoes, and prosciutto. Place the rack about 4 inches from the heating element.

Beat the eggs in a bowl until well blended, seasoning them with pepper.

Heat the olive oil in a 10-inch cast-iron or ovenproof nonstick frying pan over medium heat, swirling the pan around so that the oil coats the bottom and sides of the pan. Pour in the eggs.

As the eggs cook, lift the cooked egg from the bottom of the pan with a heat-proof rubber spatula to allow the uncooked egg to run underneath. Cook until the bottom is set and the top is still runny, 5 to 6 minutes.

Remove the pan from the heat. Sprinkle most of the cheese on top, then arrange a layer of tomatoes over the cheese, leaving a 1-inch border around the edge uncovered. Arrange the prosciutto pieces on top of the tomatoes, then sprinkle with the remaining cheese.

Place the pan under the broiler until the cheese is melted and the egg is cooked through, about 3 minutes. The edges should be puffy and golden brown. Serve warm or at room temperature.

[**NOTE:** Fontina is a creamy, mild, semifirm Italian cheese. If it's not available, you can substitute mozzarella or Monterey Jack cheese.]

PER SERVING: 395 calories, 30 g protein, 5 g carbohydrate, 29 g fat (10 g saturated), 568 mg cholesterol, 681 mg sodium, 1 g fiber

TIP: If you layer the topping carefully, leaving a wide border around the edge, the eggs will fluff up under the broiler and turn golden and crusty.

Hangtown Fry

This classic Northern California dish is named for the gold-mining town of Placerville, sometimes known as Hangtown, where newly rich gold miners would indulge in this decadent breakfast. In this rich and delicious version, the oysters are lightly breaded in cornmeal and pan-fried, then folded into a fluffy, bacon-enhanced scramble. Serve it with sourdough toast and sliced fresh fruit. (See photo on page 21.)

Heat the vegetable oil in a large frying pan over medium-high heat.

Combine the flour, cornmeal, 1 teaspoon of the salt, and a few grindings of pepper in a shallow dish. One by one, shake off the excess moisture from the oysters, then dredge in the flour mixture, thoroughly coating them.

When the oil is very hot, carefully add the oysters and fry until golden brown on one side, about 3 minutes. Turn the oysters over and fry until completely golden, about 2 minutes more. Transfer to paper towels to drain, reserving the oil in the pan.

While the oysters are frying, cook the bacon in a large nonstick frying pan over medium heat for 8 to 10 minutes, until just crisp.

Meanwhile, in a bowl, whisk together the eggs, milk, the remaining ¼ teaspoon salt, and a few grindings of pepper.

Drain off the bacon fat but leave the bacon in the pan. Add 1 to 2 tablespoons of the oil from the oysters to the bacon. Heat the pan briefly over medium heat, then add the egg mixture. Scramble, stirring constantly until just set, about 3 minutes. Remove the pan from the heat and fold in the oysters. Serve at once.

[**NOTE:** Use shucked oysters sold in jars in the refrigerated section of seafood departments rather than canned oysters.]

30 minutes

Serves 4

1	cup vegetable oil
½	cup all-purpose flour
¼	cup cornmeal
1¼	teaspoons salt
	Freshly ground pepper to taste
10	fresh jarred oysters, halved if large
6	slices bacon, diced
10	large eggs
1	cup low-fat milk

PER SERVING: 464 calories, 33 g protein, 20 g carbohydrate, 27 g fat (7 g saturated), 607 mg cholesterol, 945 mg sodium, 0 g fiber

Pasta Frittata with Zucchini

40 minutes

Serves 4

- 6 large eggs, lightly beaten
- ⅓ cup grated Parmesan cheese
- ¼ teaspoon salt, plus more to taste

  Freshly ground pepper to taste

  About 4 cups leftover cooked pasta (from 8 ounces uncooked), cold or at room temperature
- 3 tablespoons olive oil
- ¼ teaspoon dried thyme, or 1 scant teaspoon chopped fresh thyme
- 1 shallot, minced
- 2 zucchini, julienned
- ½ pint cherry tomatoes, halved
- 2 to 3 ounces fresh goat cheese

This frittata is a great way to use up leftover pasta, even if it has been in the refrigerator for a number of days. When the pasta is tossed with egg and sautéed vegetables and topped with fresh goat cheese and cherry tomatoes, it is transformed into a satisfying casserole.

Preheat the broiler, placing the rack about 4 inches from the heating element.

Combine the eggs, half of the Parmesan, ¼ teaspoon salt, and pepper in a large bowl. Stir in the pasta to coat.

Heat 1 tablespoon of the olive oil in an ovenproof nonstick frying pan over medium-low heat. Add the thyme and the shallot and sauté until tender, about 3 minutes. (If using fresh thyme, wait to add it with the zucchini.) Increase the heat to medium and add the zucchini. Sauté, stirring often, until tender and browned, 3 to 5 minutes. Season with salt and pepper.

Add the vegetables to the pasta mixture and toss quickly so that the hot vegetables don't cause the egg to cook.

Heat the remaining 2 tablespoons oil in the pan over medium heat until almost smoking, then add the pasta mixture. Cook, occasionally shaking the pan (but do not stir), until the mixture is mostly set but still a little moist on top, 4 to 5 minutes.

Distribute the tomatoes on top of the frittata, dot with the goat cheese, and sprinkle with the remaining Parmesan.

Place under the broiler until the egg is cooked through and the frittata is browned on top, about 5 minutes. Serve warm or at room temperature.

> **NOTE:** You can use any kind of leftover cooked pasta for this dish, even if it is coated with a light tomato sauce, with the exception of very large types like rigatoni.

PER SERVING: 505 calories, 23 g protein, 46 g carbohydrate, 25 g fat (8 g saturated), 332 mg cholesterol, 574 mg sodium, 5 g fiber

TIP: To julienne a vegetable, slice into thin strips about ⅛ by ⅛ by 1 to 2 inches in length.

30 minutes

Serves 4

8	small corn tortillas
1	tablespoon plus 1 teaspoon vegetable oil, plus more as needed
1/2	onion, chopped, plus minced onion for serving
1	fresh jalapeño chile, seeded and finely chopped
1/2	chipotle chile in adobo, seeded and chopped
1	14 1/2-ounce can chopped tomatoes
1/2	cup low-sodium chicken broth
	Salt to taste
8	large eggs
1/2	cup crumbled queso fresco or grated Monterey Jack cheese
	Minced fresh cilantro for serving

Huevos Rancheros

The quick ranchero sauce in this recipe has a slight kick, but the runny yolks from the eggs cooked sunny side up mellow it out considerably. Topped with crumbled queso fresco and chopped cilantro, this dish makes a great dinner served with refried black beans on the side. Serve with additional warmed tortillas.

Preheat the oven to 250°F. Place dinner plates in the oven to warm. Stack the tortillas, wrap tightly in aluminum foil, and place in the oven to warm.

Heat 1 tablespoon of the oil in a sauté pan over medium heat. Add the chopped onion and sauté until lightly browned, about 5 minutes. Add the jalapeño, chipotle chile, tomatoes with their juice, and the broth to the pan. Simmer until some of the liquid evaporates, 8 to 10 minutes. Season with salt.

Heat 1 teaspoon of the oil in a nonstick frying pan and crack 2 eggs next to each other in the pan. (If possible, use 2 pans or a large griddle to cook as many eggs as possible at a time.) Sprinkle with salt and fry over medium to medium-high heat until the whites are set, 2 to 3 minutes. Remove to one of the warmed plates and cover with foil to keep warm. Repeat with remaining eggs, adding oil to the pan as needed.

Take the tortillas out of the oven and arrange 2, slightly overlapping, on each warmed plate. Top the tortillas with 2 eggs, then ladle the ranchero sauce on top. Sprinkle with the crumbled cheese, minced onion, and cilantro, and serve.

NOTE: Chipotle chiles are dried and smoked jalapeños. They are sold canned in adobo sauce. Queso fresco is a fresh, mild Mexican cheese. Both are available in large supermarkets or from Latin American grocers.

PER SERVING: 369 calories, 19 g protein, 33 g carbohydrate, 18 g fat (5 g saturated), 431 mg cholesterol, 337 mg sodium, 4 g fiber

TIP: The hottest parts of chile peppers are the seeds, membrane, and stem, so remove these for a milder flavor. To seed a jalapeño, cut it into quarters lengthwise, then cut out the seeds and membrane from each quarter in one long slice and discard. To avoid a painful burning sensation, be careful not to touch your face or rub your eyes while handling chiles, and wash your hands—and your cutting board—thoroughly after handling them.

Fresh Vegetable Chilaquiles with Eggs

Traditional recipes for chilaquiles—a Mexican dish of leftover tortillas combined with salsa, cheese, and, sometimes, meat—don't always include eggs, but I like to add them because they make the dish lighter and fluffier. The tortillas are typically deep-fried, but here I quickly sauté them to reduce the amount of fat as well as the preparation time.

Heat the oil in a large, preferably nonstick, frying pan over medium-high heat. When hot, add the tortilla wedges and sauté until slightly browned on the bottom, about 2 minutes. Flip the tortillas over and brown the other side, about 2 minutes more. They won't all fit in one layer or be equally browned. Remove from the pan with a slotted spatula.

Add the jalapeño, onion, and zucchini to the pan and sauté, stirring occasionally, until crisp-tender, 5 to 6 minutes. Reduce heat and add the corn, tomato, and chiles to the pan and cook gently for 2 minutes. Season with salt and pepper.

Add the eggs, tortillas wedges, and half of the cheese to the vegetable mixture. Stir gently to combine, allow the eggs to set, then stir a bit to scramble until the eggs are no longer wet and shiny. Sprinkle in the remaining cheese and season again with salt and pepper. Serve at once, passing the hot sauce at the table.

30 minutes

Serves 2-3

- 1½ tablespoons vegetable oil
- 5 small corn tortillas, each cut into 8 wedges
- 1 jalapeño chile, seeded and sliced (see Tip, page 26)
- ½ onion, diced
- 1 zucchini, diced
- ½ cup frozen corn, prepared according to package directions
- 1 ripe tomato, diced
- 3 tablespoons canned diced green chiles
- Salt and freshly ground pepper to taste
- 3 large eggs, lightly beaten
- ½ cup grated Monterey Jack cheese
- Hot sauce for serving

PER SERVING: 375 calories, 16 g protein, 38 g carbohydrate, 19 g fat (6 g saturated), 229 mg cholesterol, 215 mg sodium, 6 g fiber

Hearty Soups and Stews

When made entirely from scratch, soups and stews can be a lot of work. Their recipes often require peeling and chopping up a bunch of vegetables, perhaps deboning a chicken, then simmering the results for hours. Making soups and stews might be homey, but it's difficult to find the time to do it.

Luckily, it's easy to make wholesome, comforting soups and stews quickly using store-bought chicken or vegetable broth, as long as you throw a few fresh vegetables into the pot. Adding some protein such as chicken breast, beans, or tofu turns the soup into an entrée, and offered with some French bread, tortillas, or corn bread on the side, it serves as a complete meal.

Canned beans and dried lentils are ideal ingredients for making quick main-course soups, especially when you partially puree the beans to achieve a satisfying, chunky texture. A crunchy garnish such as thick-cut tortilla chips, croutons, or homemade cheese toasts also adds some variety to both brothy soups and heartier stews. And to intensify the flavor of a simple vegetable soup, consider topping it with caramelized onions or rosemary-infused olive oil, which will draw your family to the table with an irresistible fragrance.

Facing page: Tiny Pasta Soup with Swiss Chard (recipe on page 34); Cumin–Black Bean Soup (recipe on page 31)

20 minutes

Serves 4

6 cups miso soup,
prepared according
to package directions

1 teaspoon honey

1 1-inch piece
fresh ginger

8 ounces medium-firm
tofu, cubed

2 handsful pre-washed
baby spinach

2 large eggs, lightly
beaten

Japanese Egg Drop Soup

This version of Japanese egg drop soup is a light vegetarian dish with the nurturing flavors of ginger and honey. Most Japanese egg drop soups contain dashi, a stock flavored with dried fish and seaweed, but here I use miso because it is more readily available. Medium-firm tofu is a little wobbly when you try to cut it, but it has a lovely silky texture that pairs well with the delicate swirls of egg.

Combine the miso soup and the honey in a saucepan and bring to a simmer. Peel the ginger and grate finely, then gather it into a ball and squeeze the juices into the broth.

Right before serving, bring the soup to a boil and add the tofu and the spinach, stirring until the spinach is wilted. Return the soup to a boil, then remove from heat. Using a chopstick, gently stir the soup in a circular motion in one direction. Add the egg in a thin stream as you begin to stir the soup in the opposite direction to form swirls of cooked egg, and serve.

NOTE: Miso is a fermented soybean paste that is frequently used in Japanese soups and other dishes. Look for fresh miso soup base refrigerated in the natural foods section of many supermarkets, or use instant miso soup mix.

PER SERVING: 140 calories, 11 g protein, 11 g carbohydrate, 7 g fat (1 g saturated), 105 mg cholesterol, 812 mg sodium, 2 g fiber

TIP: To peel ginger, cut off a piece the size you want, then use a paring knife to trim off any small knobs so that you have a relatively smooth oblong piece. Use the edge of a sturdy soup spoon to scrape off the thin, papery peel.

Cumin-Black Bean Soup

When I was in college my roommate Nora and I often made easy dishes from a book of recipes that her mother had put together. One of those recipes was for a warming black bean soup that only required chopping up a few vegetables and opening a can of beans, a can of broth, and a can of tomatoes. This recipe is almost as simple, but it's spiced up with cumin and red pepper flakes. Sour cream tames the heat, but you can also cut the quantity of red pepper flakes in half, if you like. Serve with corn bread. (See photo on page 29.)

Heat the vegetable oil in a heavy stockpot or saucepan over medium heat. Add the onion, carrots, cumin, and red pepper flakes and sauté until the onions are tender, 10 minutes.

Add the broth, the beans and their liquid, the orange juice, salt, and pepper. Bring to a boil, then reduce the heat to a simmer and cook until the carrots are tender and the flavors are combined, 5 minutes.

Using an immersion or regular blender, puree the soup until it is mostly smooth but still has some texture. Serve at once, passing the sour cream at the table.

30 minutes

Serves 4

1	tablespoon vegetable oil
1	onion, chopped
2	carrots, peeled and finely diced
2	teaspoons ground cumin
1	teaspoon red pepper flakes
1	quart low-sodium vegetable broth
2½	15-ounce cans black beans, with their liquid
½	cup orange juice
1 to 2	teaspoons salt, or to taste
	Freshly ground black pepper
	About ¼ cup low-fat sour cream or plain yogurt

PER SERVING: 291 calories, 15 g protein, 45 g carbohydrate, 7 g fat (1 g saturated), 6 mg cholesterol, 1,328 mg sodium, 15 g fiber

1 28-ounce can peeled
   whole tomatoes

½ small red onion,
   coarsely chopped

1 large cucumber,
   peeled and thickly
   sliced

2 serrano chiles, with
   seeds and membranes
   removed (see Tip,
   page 26)

3 tablespoons extra
   virgin olive oil

1 tablespoon red wine
   vinegar or sherry
   vinegar

   Salt and freshly
   ground pepper
   to taste

   Pinch of cayenne
   pepper, if needed

1 to 2 slices day-old French
   or Italian bread, torn
   into pieces, if needed

½ firm but ripe avocado,
   cubed

1 gold, orange, or green
   heirloom tomato,
   diced (optional)

Gazpacho with Avocado

Traditional gazpacho, a chilled Spanish soup made with fresh, ripe summer tomatoes, is delicious but time-consuming to prepare. Surprisingly, canned tomatoes work almost as well as fresh, as long as you use good-quality whole peeled tomatoes (I like Muir Glen organic brand and San Marzano tomatoes from Italy). Vinegar and chiles help intensify the soup's simple but fresh flavors, and a generous sprinkling of salt also brings out the taste of the vegetables. Serve with quesadillas for a main course. It also makes an easy first course for a dinner party.

Place the tomatoes with about half of their juice in a blender. Reserve the remaining juice. Add the onion, cucumber, serrano chiles, olive oil, vinegar, salt, and pepper, and puree until smooth. Taste and adjust the seasoning, adding a pinch of cayenne and more salt if needed to bring out the flavor.

If the soup seems too thin, add 1 slice of the bread and puree again until it is thoroughly incorporated. Check the soup's consistency. If it is still too thin, repeat with the remaining slice of bread. If, however, it is too thick, add the rest of the tomato juice and pulse briefly. Taste and adjust the seasoning again.

Refrigerate until cold, at least a few hours or up to overnight, or pour into a bowl and "flash-chill" (see Tip below).

To serve, divide the soup among serving bowls and top with the diced heirloom tomato, if using it, and the avocado.

PER SERVING: 185 calories,
3 g protein, 14 g carbohydrate,
14 g fat (2 g saturated),
0 mg cholesterol, 298 mg sodium,
3 g fiber

TIP: To cube avocado, cut it in half and remove the pit. Without cutting through the skin, score the avocado half in a crisscross pattern, then scoop out the cubes with a large spoon. To "flash-chill" this dish, place in a bowl in the freezer, stirring frequently so the food at the edge of the bowl doesn't freeze, until cold, 20-30 minutes.

35 minutes

Serves 4

About ⅓ pound tiny pasta (pastina)

16 thin slices baguette, cut on an angle

¼ cup pre-grated pecorino or Parmesan cheese

1 large bunch Swiss chard

2 tablespoons extra virgin olive oil

4 cloves garlic, peeled and lightly crushed

Pinch of red pepper flakes

3 cups low-sodium vegetable or chicken broth

Salt and freshly ground pepper to taste

Tiny Pasta Soup with Swiss Chard

In Italy, the equivalent of a comforting bowl of chicken noodle soup is pasta in brodo, or a brothy soup made with various types of tiny pasta shapes, called pastina. Look for pasta with names like acini di pepe (peppercorns), pastina, riso (rice), semi di melone (melon seeds), or orzo. (See photo on page 28.)

Preheat the broiler, placing the rack about 4 inches from the heating element. Bring a large pot of salted water to a boil for the pasta. When the water reaches a boil, cook the pasta according to the package instructions until it is al dente. Drain, reserving 2 cups of the cooking water.

Meanwhile, place the baguette slices on a baking sheet and top each slice with an equal amount of the cheese. Broil until the bread is toasted and the cheese is browned, 1 minute. Watch carefully, as the cheese can burn quickly.

Pull the leaves off the chard and discard the stems. Stack the leaves, then slice them crosswise into thin ribbons.

Heat the olive oil in a large, heavy stockpot over medium heat. Add the garlic and red pepper flakes and cook until the garlic begins to release its aroma, 1 to 2 minutes. Stir in the chard and cook for a few minutes to wilt. Add the broth, bring to a simmer, cover, and cook until the chard is tender, about 5 minutes.

Add the cooked pasta and the reserved pasta-cooking water to the stockpot and heat through. The mixture should be quite soupy. Season with salt and pepper. To serve, ladle the soup into bowls and top with the cheese toasts.

PER SERVING: 359 calories, 13 g protein, 48 g carbohydrate, 13 g fat (3 g saturated), 8 mg cholesterol, 442 mg sodium, 4 g fiber

Lentil & Arugula Soup
with Caramelized Onion

To caramelize onions, they are typically cooked over low heat for up to an hour. In this recipe you cook them for only 20 minutes at a medium-high temperature, but they still provide a sweet, intense dimension to this simple lentil soup. Stirring in arugula at the end adds bright green color and fresh flavor.

Combine the lentils, broth, and 2 cups water in a saucepan. Cover and bring to a boil. Reduce the heat to a simmer and simmer steadily for 20 minutes, occasionally skimming the scum from the surface with a large spoon.

Meanwhile, melt the butter in a large, heavy frying pan over medium-high heat. When it foams, add the onions and sauté, stirring often, until they take on a deep golden-brown color, about 20 minutes. Watch the onions carefully and adjust the heat if necessary so that they do not burn.

Meanwhile, peel and finely dice the carrots. Add the carrots to the lentils and return to a simmer.

When the lentils have cooked for 20 minutes, add ½ to 1 teaspoon salt, depending on the saltiness of the broth, and simmer until the lentils are tender but still have a bit of texture and the carrots are soft, another 5 to 10 minutes.

When the onions have reached a deep golden-brown color, add the vinegar, sugar, and a few tablespoons water. Deglaze the pan, stirring to scrape up any bits that may have stuck to the bottom. Season the onions with salt and pepper, remove from the heat, and set aside.

Right before serving, add the arugula to the soup and simmer just until wilted. Season with pepper. To serve, ladle the soup into serving bowls and top with the caramelized onions.

> **NOTE:** French green lentils, or lentilles du Puy, remain firmer when cooked than the larger regular green lentils. Their cooking time can vary, though, so make sure you cook them until they are tender to the bite but still have some texture.

TIP: To save time when making this dish, first start cooking the lentils, then slice and begin browning the onions. Once these ingredients are on the stovetop you can start peeling and chopping the carrots, then quickly add them to the lentils.

35 minutes

Serves 4

- 1 cup French or regular green lentils
- 1 quart low-sodium vegetable or chicken broth
- 2 tablespoons unsalted butter, cut into pieces
- 2 onions, thinly sliced
- 2 carrots
- ½ to 1 teaspoon salt, plus more to taste
- 2 tablespoons red wine vinegar
- Pinch of sugar
- Freshly ground pepper to taste
- 1 small bunch arugula, coarsely chopped

PER SERVING: 259 calories, 16 g protein, 37 g carbohydrate, 6 g fat (4 g saturated), 15 mg cholesterol, 945 mg sodium, 10 g fiber

25 minutes

Serves 4

20 frozen gyoza
or pot stickers

6 cups low-sodium
chicken broth

1 small bunch kale or
chard, or ½ bunch
napa cabbage, stems
removed and leaves
cut into ribbons (about
4 cups chopped)

1 tablespoon reduced-
sodium soy sauce

1 cup frozen shelled
edamame or peas

1 sheet nori

Gyoza Soup with Edamame & Toasted Nori

Pot stickers and their Japanese version, gyoza, delicate wrappers plump with savory filling, are perfect little bundles of food. Although nothing beats freshly made dumplings, the frozen variety work well in soup recipes such as this one. Dumplings specifically labeled gyoza work even better than pot stickers in soups because they are smaller and tend to have thinner wrappers.

Bring 8 cups of water to a boil in a covered stockpot, then cook the gyoza according to the package directions and drain.

Meanwhile, bring the broth and 3 cups water to a boil in another large, covered pot. Add the greens and soy sauce. Cook until the greens are tender, about 10 minutes for kale or 5 minutes for the chard or cabbage. Add the edamame and cook for the amount of time called for on the package.

Using tongs, hold the nori over the low flame of a gas stove burner until lightly toasted all over. It should turn a burnished green and become crisp and fragrant. If you don't have a gas stove, toast in a dry frying pan. Crumble the toasted nori into bite-size pieces.

To serve, ladle the soup into serving bowls, then top with the pot stickers. Garnish with the toasted nori just before serving.

NOTE: Nori, pressed sheets of dried seaweed, is found in the Asian food aisle of most supermarkets. Though most people are familiar with nori because it's used to make sushi, it also adds a clean, wholesome flavor and extra nutrients to dishes such as this simple soup.

PER SERVING: 405 calories,
26 g protein, 56 g carbohydrate,
9 g fat (2 g saturated),
36 mg cholesterol,
812 mg sodium, 6 g fiber

35 minutes

Serves 4 to 5

SOUP

- 1 large bunch dino kale or other type of kale
- 3 cloves garlic, minced
- 2 carrots, peeled and diced
- 1 small onion, chopped
- 2 15-ounce cans Great Northern, cannellini, or other white beans, rinsed and drained
- 1 teaspoon salt
- ½ teaspoon freshly ground pepper

GARNISH

- ½ cup extra virgin olive oil
- 1 large sprig fresh rosemary

  Croutons
- ½ cup grated Parmesan cheese

White Bean & Kale Soup with Rosemary Oil

This hearty vegetarian soup is a great way to use up kale when it is in season. The rosemary oil, which you prepare by quickly simmering a sprig of rosemary in olive oil, gives the soup an extra jolt of flavor and a wonderful aroma that you'll enjoy as you take your first spoonful. If you can't find canned or jarred white beans, chickpeas would work, too, though the texture of the soup won't be as smooth.

To make the soup, pull the leaves off the kale and discard the stems. Stack the leaves, then slice them crosswise into ribbons ½ inch wide. Place the kale in a stockpot with the garlic, carrots, onion, beans, salt, pepper, and 6 cups water. Bring to a boil, stir to submerge the greens, then reduce the heat to a simmer and cover. Simmer the soup until the kale and other vegetables are very tender but not mushy, 20 minutes.

Using an immersion or regular blender, puree the soup until it is mostly smooth but still has some texture.

To make the garnish, while the soup cooks, place the olive oil in a small saucepan with the rosemary sprig over low heat and warm until the oil is fragrant, 5 to 10 minutes. Remove the rosemary sprig from the oil and discard or break into pieces and use to garnish each bowl of soup.

To serve, ladle the soup into bowls, top with the croutons and cheese, and drizzle with the rosemary oil to taste.

[**NOTE:** Dino kale, which supposedly got its name because its long, narrow leaves look like reptilian skin, is an heirloom variety also known as Tuscan kale, black kale or cavolo nero (black cabbage).]

PER SERVING: 271 calories, 13 g protein, 31 g carbohydrate, 15 g fat (3 g saturated), 6 mg cholesterol, 1,088 mg sodium, 8 g fiber

TIP: Any leftover rosemary oil can be kept in the refrigerator for a few days and used in a salad dressing. This soup also freezes well, so double the recipe, including the 6 cups water, if you'd like to have more for later. Serve the leftovers with fresh rosemary oil, croutons, and Parmesan.

Noodle Bowl with Shrimp, Broccolini & Shallot Crisps

Many different Asian cultures have their own version of noodles in a bowl of broth. This soup features plump shrimp, crispy shallot slices for texture, and fresh broccolini. Broccolini is a sweet, fast-cooking hybrid of asparagus and Chinese broccoli. If you prefer, you can substitute bite-size pieces of regular broccoli.

Bring a large pot of water to a boil for the noodles.

Combine the broth and soy sauce in a saucepan and bring to a simmer. Add the ginger to the broth. Cover and adjust the heat to maintain a simmer while you fry the shallots.

Pour the vegetable oil in a small saucepan to a depth of about 1 inch. Heat over medium-high heat until a shallot slice dropped into the oil sizzles. When it reaches the correct temperature, add all of the shallot slices to the oil and fry, stirring often, until golden brown, about 2 minutes. Remove the shallots from the oil with a slotted spoon and drain on paper towels.

Cook the noodles according to the package directions. Drain the noodles and mound them in large, deep bowls.

Add the broccolini to the broth and cover. Increase the heat so the broth reaches a low boil and cook until crisp-tender, 1 to 2 minutes. Add the shrimp to the broth and cook until just curled and pink, 1 to 2 minutes.

With a slotted spoon, remove the ginger from the broth. Pour the broth, broccolini, and shrimp on top of the noodles. Drizzle with a few drops of chile oil, if using, and top with the shallot crisps. Serve at once.

[
NOTE: You can find fresh noodles labeled "Asian-style" in the produce section of many supermarkets.
]

20 minutes

Serves 4

- 6 cups low-sodium chicken broth
- 2 tablespoons soy sauce
- 1 2-inch piece fresh ginger, unpeeled and sliced into coins
- About 1/2 cup vegetable oil
- 1 shallot, very thinly sliced
- 2 9-ounce packages fresh wide-cut Asian-style noodles
- 1 pound broccolini, cut into 2-inch pieces
- 1 pound peeled and deveined medium shrimp (see Note, page 103)
- Red chile oil to taste (optional)

PER SERVING: 576 calories, 46 g protein, 80 g carbohydrate, 8 g fat (2 g saturated), 326 mg cholesterol, 549 mg sodium, 6 g fiber

30 minutes

Serves 4

4 ounces rice stick noodles, broken into large pieces

1 pound boneless, skinless chicken breasts, cut into ½- by 1-inch pieces

2 teaspoons soy sauce

3 stalks lemongrass

1½ tablespoons vegetable oil

1-inch piece fresh ginger, peeled and finely grated (see Tip, page 30)

1 quart low-sodium chicken broth

1 13½-ounce can coconut milk

1 tablespoon fresh lime juice (from about ½ lime)

1½ tablespoons Asian fish sauce

1 cup bean sprouts, plus more for garnish

6 sprigs fresh cilantro

Chicken Noodle Soup with Lemongrass & Coconut Milk

When you're ill or feeling blue, make a pot of this soup, which is inspired by the Thai soup tom yum gai. The fragrance of lemongrass, ginger, and cilantro wafting from the bowl will lift your spirits better than any aromatherapy treatment could. The broth, though rich with coconut milk, has a citrus tang.

Place the rice stick noodles in a large bowl and cover with hot water. Let soak while you prepare the other ingredients.

Place the chicken in a bowl, drizzle with the soy sauce, and stir to coat the chicken pieces.

Using the side of a large knife, crush the bulbous ends of the lemongrass stalks. Cut off the thin ends if necessary so that the stalks will fit into a stockpot.

Heat the oil in a stockpot over medium heat. Add the lemongrass and ginger and sauté until fragrant, 2 to 3 minutes. Increase the heat to medium-high and add the chicken. Sauté, stirring constantly, until chicken just turns white, about 2 minutes. Add the chicken broth, coconut milk, lime juice, and fish sauce. Bring to a boil.

Drain the rice stick noodles and add them to the pot. Simmer until the noodles are completely soft and the chicken is cooked through, 3 to 5 minutes. Remove the lemongrass from the pot and discard. Add the bean sprouts and heat through.

To serve, ladle into large bowls and garnish with cilantro and additional bean sprouts.

NOTE: Rice stick noodles are very thin dried rice noodles available in the Asian foods aisle of supermarkets. If they are unavailable, substitute with bean thread noodles. Fresh lemongrass is found in many supermarket produce sections. Seek out fresh-looking stalks with thick bulbs, which are the most fragrant part of the vegetable.

PER SERVING: 515 calories, 34 g protein, 30 g carbohydrate, 29 g fat (21 g saturated), 65 mg cholesterol, 1,291 mg sodium, 1 g fiber

20 minutes

Serves 4

1   15-ounce can black beans, drained and rinsed

1   quart low-sodium chicken broth

Salt to taste

8   ounces boneless, skinless chicken thighs or breasts, diced

1   cup fresh or frozen corn kernels

1   6-ounce bag thick-cut tortilla chips

1   avocado, cubed (see Tip, page 32)

1½   cups fresh roasted-tomato or tomatillo salsa

Fresh cilantro leaves for garnish (optional)

Lime wedges for garnish (optional)

Jalapeño chile slices for garnish (optional)

PER SERVING: 515 calories, 28 g protein, 57 g carbohydrate, 22 g fat (4 g saturated), 34 mg cholesterol, 833 mg sodium, 12 g fiber

Tortilla Soup with Chicken

This easy version of a traditional Mexican soup uses salsa made from roasted tomatillos or tomatoes. Although the optional garnishes will probably repeat the flavors featured in the salsa, they make the soup look pretty.

Combine the beans, broth and 2 cups water in a large pot. Bring to a simmer, then taste and add salt until the broth is salty enough for your liking (the broth will season the chicken as it cooks). Add the chicken and corn. Return to a simmer and cook gently until chicken is cooked through, about 7 minutes.

Meanwhile, break up the tortilla chips into large pieces and divide among 4 soup bowls. Distribute the avocado cubes in four serving bowls.

Remove the pot from the heat, add 1 cup of the salsa, and taste. Add up to ½ cup more salsa, depending on how spicy you like it. Return the pot to the heat until heated through, 1 to 2 minutes.

To serve, ladle the soup into the prepared bowls, then top with the cilantro leaves, lime wedges, and jalapeño slices, if using.

Tomatillo Chili with Pork

Influenced by chile verde, the tangy Mexican pork stew flavored with tomatillos and green chiles, this dish uses quick-cooking ground pork instead of stew meat and contains prepared salsa verde, or green salsa, for instant flavor. And although chile verde doesn't contain beans, you'll discover that the beans taste great. Serve with warm tortillas or corn bread, or over long-grain rice.

Heat a Dutch oven over high heat for a few minutes, then add the oil. When the oil is hot but not smoking, add the pork in large clumps. Sprinkle with salt and pepper. Brown undisturbed for a minute or two, then turn to brown the other side. Using a spatula, break into 1-inch chunks. Remove with a slotted spoon and set aside.

Reduce the heat to medium-low and add the garlic and tomatillos. Brown for a minute or two, then add the broth, pinto beans, salsa verde, and pork. Adjust the heat to a steady simmer, then cook, covered, until the tomatillos have softened, 15 minutes. Uncover and continue simmering until the liquid thickens, about 5 minutes. Taste and adjust the seasoning with salt and pepper, if needed. Ladle into bowls and serve at once.

[**NOTE:** Tomatillos, which are small, green members of the tomato family with a papery husk, are available in Latin American markets and many supermarkets.]

35 minutes

Serves 4

- 2 teaspoons vegetable oil
- 1 pound ground pork (see Note, page 144)

  Salt and freshly ground pepper to taste
- 3 cloves garlic, minced
- 12 ounces tomatillos, hulled, rinsed, and quartered
- 1 14-ounce can low-sodium chicken broth
- 1 15-ounce can pinto beans, rinsed and drained
- 1 7-ounce can spicy salsa verde

PER SERVING: 466 calories, 28 g protein, 24 g carbohydrate, 28 g fat (9 g saturated), 82 mg cholesterol, 448 mg sodium, 7 g fiber

Making the Perfect Vinaigrette

A plain salad made with nothing but lettuce can be delicious if you achieve the right balance of acid and oil in the dressing, and it's easier to achieve this balance if the dressing is emulsified, or the oil and vinegar are smoothly combined into a satiny mixture.

To make an emulsified dressing, curl a damp dishtowel into a circle, place it on the kitchen counter, and rest a bowl on top so that it will remain steady while you whisk. Whisk together the vinegar or other acidic ingredient with the salt, pepper, and herbs or spices you are using until the salt has dissolved (the salt will dissolve more easily in the dressing before you add the oil).

With the whisk in one hand and the bottle of oil in the other, begin drizzling a few drops of oil into the dressing while whisking. When the oil begins to be evenly distributed, start pouring more oil in a thin, steady stream, whisking vigorously all the while, until the vinaigrette is slightly creamy and thick.

Taste the vinaigrette with a lettuce leaf. If the acid still burns a little in the back of your throat, whisk in more oil. If it tastes too fatty, add more vinegar. Season with salt and pepper, if needed, before using to dress your salad greens.

Lentil Salad with Tomatoes & Feta Cheese (recipe on page 46)

Main Course Salads

*Achiote Chicken with Jicama Salad
(recipe on page 58)*

A salad seems as if it should be one of the easiest things to make—all it should take is a fistful of lettuce, a dice of tomato, a drizzle of vinaigrette. But whether it's a plate of delicate baby greens served at an upscale restaurant or a Caesar salad in a bag purchased from the supermarket, salads often go all wrong. Sometimes the greens are wilted and dripping with oil, the dressing is puckery with acid, or some of the ingredients are too heavy and slide off the lettuce into a watery puddle.

Making a good salad requires bringing all of the ingredients into balance. A salad should be light and cleansing but also offer a satisfying juxtaposition of textures. The flavors should dance around one another.

Heavy ingredients can wilt delicate greens and end up at the bottom of the salad bowl, especially in main course salads. That's why I like to pair items such as shredded chicken or smoked trout with hearty greens such as romaine lettuce, and to cut salad ingredients into similar-size pieces.

Here are a few more tips for creating a salad with a sense of harmony:

• Dry the greens thoroughly. Water left on lettuce or other ingredients can break the dressing's emulsion and prevent it from delicately clinging to the greens. Invest in a good salad spinner and spin the lettuce leaves until they are quite dry (this usually requires three rounds of vigorous spinning). Pour off the water between each round.

• Dress the greens in moderation. Add the dressing a little at a time as you toss the salad, tasting individual leaves as you go to determine when you have achieved a light, even coating.

• Season the salad. The flavor of fresh lettuce really shines through when you add a pinch of salt and pepper to the finished salad, even if the dressing is already seasoned.

35 minutes

Serves 4

1½ teaspoons salt,
    plus more to taste

1   cup French or
    regular green lentils

    Leaves from 3 sprigs
    fresh mint

5   teaspoons
    champagne vinegar,
    or 3 tablespoons
    white wine vinegar

    Freshly ground pepper
    to taste

2   tablespoons extra
    virgin olive oil

1 to 2 hearts of romaine

1   vine-ripened tomato,
    cored and diced,
    or 1 cup halved cherry
    tomatoes

5   ounces crumbled feta
    or fresh goat cheese

Lentil Salad
with Tomatoes & Feta Cheese

Too often, lentils are cooked to a mush and taste muddy, but you can avoid these pitfalls, especially if you seek out small French green lentils, also called lentilles du Puy. Smaller and rounder than the common green or brown lentils, these delicate specimens keep their firm, pebbly shape after being cooked and have a pleasing toothsomeness. (Regular green lentils, however, will also work just fine in this recipe.) Lentils' natural earthiness is wonderful juxtaposed with rich feta cheese, tangy champagne vinegar, and cool, refreshing mint. (See photo on page 44.)

Bring 2 quarts of water and the 1½ teaspoons salt to a boil in a saucepan. Add the lentils and return to a boil. Reduce the heat and simmer until the lentils are cooked through but still firm, about 25 minutes. Drain, then cool the lentils by rinsing with cool running water. Drain thoroughly in a colander for a few minutes.

Meanwhile, cut the mint leaves into chiffonade: stack the leaves, gently roll them up, then thinly slice across the roll to form thin ribbons. Set aside.

Combine the vinegar, pepper, and salt to taste in a large bowl and whisk to combine. Slowly drizzle in the olive oil, whisking constantly, to form an emulsified vinaigrette (see page 44).

Separate the heart of romaine into individual leaves. Divide these among serving plates, with the narrower parts of the leaves pointing toward the center of the plate like the spokes of a wheel.

Add the lentils, tomatoes, mint, and feta to the vinaigrette in the bowl. Toss to combine, then add salt and pepper to taste. Pile the lentil mixture on top of the romaine leaves and serve.

PER SERVING: 310 calories, 16 g protein, 32 g carbohydrate, 14 g fat (6 g saturated), 32 mg cholesterol, 47 mg sodium, 8 g fiber

TIP: Served with bread, this salad makes a perfect light dinner or lunch; add diced prosciutto, cooked chicken, or tofu for a heartier meal. This salad is also great for parties. Make it ahead and refrigerate, then place in a large serving bowl with the romaine leaves sticking out. Guests can use the leaves to scoop up the salad.

Cabbage Slaw
with Avocado & Pepitas

This Cal-Mex salad is one of my personal favorites. The avocado and pepitas make this salad hearty enough to serve as a vegetarian main course, but it's also great with grilled steak or chicken, cut into thin slices. It may be made a few hours ahead, but wait until just before serving to add the pepitas and avocado.

To make the vinaigrette, whisk together all the ingredients except the oil. Let the cilantro steep in the lime juice for a few minutes, then slowly drizzle in the oil, whisking constantly, to form an emulsified vinaigrette (see page 44).

To make the salad, cut the cabbage into quarters and trim away the white core with diagonal cuts. Thinly slice the leaves into ribbons, then toss the cabbage in the vinaigrette. Set the cabbage aside to marinate while you prepare the other ingredients.

Toast the pepitas in a heavy frying pan over medium-low heat until they start popping. Stir or toss frequently to avoid scorching until all the seeds are puffed up and toasty. Transfer to a bowl.

Cut the avocado in half, remove the pit, and thinly slice. Scoop out the slices with a spoon and toss with the cabbage (the lime juice in the dressing will help prevent the avocado from browning). Add the pepitas, bell peppers, and green onions and toss to combine. Season with salt, plenty of black pepper, and additional lime juice, if it needs a little more zip, and serve.

[
NOTE: Pepitas, or shelled green pumpkin seeds, are available at Latino and health food markets.
]

30 minutes

Serves 4 to 6

VINAIGRETTE

- 2 tablespoons fresh lime juice (from about 1 lime)
- ¼ cup minced fresh cilantro
- ⅛ teaspoon salt

  Freshly ground pepper to taste

  Pinch of cayenne pepper
- ¼ teaspoon sugar
- 3 tablespoons vegetable oil

SALAD

- ½ head green cabbage (about 1 pound)
- ⅓ cup pepitas
- 1 firm but ripe avocado
- 2 red bell peppers, stemmed, deribbed, and julienned (see Tip, page 24)
- 2 green onions, thinly sliced

  Salt and freshly ground pepper to taste

  Lime juice to taste

PER SERVING: 175 calories, 3 g protein, 8 g carbohydrate, 15 g fat (2 g saturated), 0 mg cholesterol, 103 mg sodium, 3 g fiber

20 minutes

Serves 6

4 1/2	tablespoons champagne or red wine vinegar
3/4	teaspoon salt
	Freshly ground pepper to taste
1/2	cup olive oil
1	pound penne rigate (see Note, page 69)
10	ounces pre-washed baby spinach
1/2	medium red onion, thinly sliced
3/4	cup walnuts, coarsely chopped
3/4 to 1	cup crumbled fresh goat cheese or blue cheese
	Seeds from 1 medium pomegranate

Spinach Salad with Pomegranates, Penne & Goat Cheese

Ruby-red pomegranate seeds and shining baby spinach leaves make this the perfect winter holiday dish, but it's great served any time of year as a light main course. When pomegranates aren't available, use about 1/2 cup dried cranberries or 1/2 pint fresh raspberries. A champagne vinaigrette adds a bright note to the sweet-tart fruit.

Bring a pot of salted water to a boil for the pasta.

Combine the vinegar, salt, and pepper in a bowl and whisk to combine. Slowly drizzle in the olive oil, whisking constantly, to form an emulsified vinaigrette (see page 44).

Add the pasta to the boiling water and cook according to the package directions.

Drain the pasta and transfer to a large salad bowl. Toss with half of the vinaigrette. Add the spinach and toss again until the leaves are wilted. Toss in the red onion, walnuts, and about two-thirds of the cheese. Drizzle on the remaining dressing as desired (you may have leftover dressing), then toss again to coat all the ingredients.

To serve, divide the salad among serving plates, then top with the pomegranate seeds and the remaining cheese. Serve warm.

TIP: To save time when making this recipe, remove the pomegranate seeds while the pasta cooks: quarter the pomegranate by lightly scoring through the skin (but not the fruit) with a paring knife. Separate into quarters by holding the fruit in a bowl of water and slowly pulling the segments apart. Working one segment at a time, use your fingers to remove the seeds under water. The white pith will float to the top while the seeds sink to the bottom, and you won't get squirted with the seeds' bright red juice. Discard the skin and pith and drain the seeds before using.

PER SERVING: 481 calories, 14 g protein, 67 g carbohydrate, 20 g fat (3 g saturated), 2 mg cholesterol, 159 mg sodium, 3 g fiber

20 minutes

Serves 6

1   pound gemelli or fusilli

3   zucchini, grated on the large holes of a grater

¼   teaspoon salt, plus more to taste

1   clove garlic, minced

3   tablespoons thinly sliced fresh basil leaves or a mix of basil, parsley and/or mint

2   tablespoons white wine vinegar

Freshly ground pepper to taste

2 to 3   tablespoons extra virgin olive oil

2   large vine-ripened tomatoes, diced, or 1 pint cherry tomatoes, halved

3   tablespoons grated Parmesan cheese

Summer Vegetable Pasta Salad

This pasta salad takes very little time to assemble, but it needs to chill for at least an hour or overnight, or by "flash chilling" (see Tip, page 32). If you make it a day in advance, wait to add the tomatoes and extra olive oil (as well as additional seasoning) until just before serving. For an extra serving of good-for-you greens, serve over a bed of baby arugula or spinach drizzled with lemon juice.

Bring a large pot of salted water to a boil. Add the pasta and cook according to the package instructions until it is al dente.

Meanwhile, place the grated zucchini in a colander and toss with the ¼ teaspoon salt. Let sit until some of the liquid drains off and the zucchini softens slightly, 5 to 10 minutes. Toss again and press down with your hands to remove some more of the moisture.

Combine in a bowl the garlic, basil, vinegar, salt, and pepper, and whisk to combine. Let sit for a minute or two for the flavors to infuse the vinegar, then slowly drizzle in 2 tablespoons of the oil, whisking constantly, to form an emulsified vinaigrette (see page 44).

When the pasta is done, drain it and rinse under cold running water, then drain again well. Place the pasta in a large bowl with the zucchini, tomatoes, and Parmesan. Add the dressing and toss until the zucchini is no longer in clumps.

Cover tightly and chill for at least 1 hour or overnight or "flash chill." Before serving, season with salt and pepper, and toss in an additional tablespoon of olive oil if the salad seems dry.

PER SERVING: 383 calories, 12 g protein, 55 g carbohydrate, 7 g fat (2 g saturated), 2 mg cholesterol, 68 mg sodium, 4 g fiber

Cool Iceberg Wedges
with Shrimp & Blue Cheese Dressing

Iceberg lettuce isn't trendy like baby mixed greens, but it is a fine ingredient when treated right. Though lacking in flavor, it has a crisp, juicy texture that comes out best when it is served ice-cold and in large wedges. When piled with croutons, hard-cooked eggs, and plump shrimp, iceberg lettuce turns into a hearty main-course salad.

Place the eggs in a small saucepan and add water to cover by 1 inch. Bring to a rolling boil and cook for 8 minutes. Remove from the heat, drain, and let cool under running water for a few minutes. When cool, peel the eggs and cut each in half.

Cut each head of lettuce into four wedges, or into eight wedges if you're using one large head of lettuce, and remove the core from each wedge with a long, diagonal cut. Place 2 wedges on each serving plate.

Combine the sour cream, mayonnaise, and lemon juice in a bowl. Stir in the blue cheese and season with pepper.

Arrange the shrimp and egg halves around the iceberg wedges, then drizzle with about half of the dressing. Divide the green onions, cherry tomatoes, and croutons among the plates, sprinkling them on top of the lettuce. Add a few grindings of pepper and serve at once, passing the remaining dressing at the table.

20 minutes

Serves 4

2	large eggs
1 to 2	heads iceberg lettuce (about 2 to 3 pounds total)
1/3	cup nonfat sour cream or plain yogurt
1/3	cup mayonnaise
1	tablespoon fresh lemon juice (from a half lemon)
1/2	cup crumbled blue cheese
	Freshly ground pepper to taste
1	pound precooked peeled medium shrimp, tails removed (see Note, page 103)
4	green onions, thinly sliced
1/2	cup cherry tomatoes, stems removed
	Garlic croutons

TIP: For the most refreshing salad, keep your dressing ingredients, shrimp, lettuce, and even serving plates chilled until the last minute. You can also serve like a traditional tossed salad, with chopped iceberg lettuce.

PER SERVING: 409 calories, 33 g protein, 16 g carbohydrate, 24 g fat (6 g saturated), 195 mg cholesterol, 696 mg sodium, 3 g fiber

20 minutes

Serves 4

12 ounces lump crabmeat or cooked bay shrimp

¼ cup mayonnaise

1½ tablespoons fresh lemon juice, plus more for drizzling (about 1 lemon total)

1 tablespoon chopped fresh Italian (flat-leaf) parsley, tarragon, or dill

Salt and freshly ground pepper to taste

4 to 6 ounces mixed baby salad greens or baby arugula

½ cucumber, thinly sliced into half moons

Olive oil for drizzling

2 large, firm but ripe avocados

Crab-Stuffed Avocado Salad

My Grandpa Art taught me how to eat an avocado: cut it in half, squirt it with ketchup, and eat it with a spoon. He worked for Del Monte Foods, which explains his condiment of choice, as well as his love of produce. As a grown-up I still love to dig into an avocado with a spoon, although salt and lemon juice now take the place of ketchup. With this recipe, you go even further and turn the delectable fruit into a main course salad with fresh crab. If crab is out of season, substitute precooked bay shrimp.

Pick through the crabmeat to remove any cartilage, setting aside a few legs to garnish the plates. Gently fold together the crabmeat, mayonnaise, lemon juice, and herbs. Season lightly with salt and pepper.

Distribute the salad greens among serving plates and top with the cucumber slices. Drizzle some lemon juice over the greens, then drizzle with a little olive oil and season with salt and pepper.

Cut the avocados in half and remove the pits, then carefully remove the peel. Place an avocado half on each bed of greens and pile the crab salad in each cavity.

Garnish the plates with the reserved crab legs and serve.

PER SERVING: 370 calories, 22 g protein, 10 g carbohydrate, 29 g fat (4 g saturated), 72 mg cholesterol, 420 mg sodium, 5 g fiber

TIP: To reduce the amount of fat in this recipe—which is mostly heart-healthy fat from the avocados—replace half of the mayonnaise with nonfat plain yogurt.

Smoked Trout Salad

Smoked trout is a nice alternative to smoked salmon. In this dish, the melt-in-your-mouth fish is offset by complex flavors and textures, including briny olives, crisp romaine, sweet red onions, nutty chickpeas, and a citrusy herb dressing. This dish makes a wonderful addition to a brunch or picnic. Serve with hearty Italian bread or throw in some croutons for a little more substance.

To make the dressing, whisk together the vinegar, lemon juice, yogurt, herbs, salt, pepper, and cayenne. Set aside for a few minutes so that the flavor of the herbs infuses the vinegar. Slowly drizzle in the olive oil, whisking constantly, to form an emulsified vinaigrette (see page 44).

To assemble the salad, combine the romaine, trout, olives, chickpeas, and onion in a large bowl. Add the dressing and toss to coat. Add more black pepper to taste. Serve at once.

TIP: Olives are delicious but have a lot of sodium and fat, so skip them if you're concerned about the amount of them in your diet.

---

25 minutes

Serves 4

DRESSING

1 tablespoon white or red wine vinegar

1 tablespoon fresh lemon juice

¼ cup nonfat plain yogurt

1 to 2 tablespoons minced fresh cilantro, tarragon, basil, or mint

Salt and freshly ground pepper to taste

Dash of cayenne pepper

3 tablespoons extra virgin olive oil

SALAD

2 hearts of romaine, cut into 1-inch strips (or 10 ounces precleaned, chopped romaine)

6 ounces smoked trout, skin removed and flesh flaked into bite-size pieces

½ cup dry- or oil-cured olives, pitted and torn into bite-size pieces

1 cup canned chickpeas, drained and rinsed

½ small red onion, thinly sliced

PER SERVING: 341 calories, 16 g protein, 16 g carbohydrate, 24 g fat (3 g saturated), 34 mg cholesterol, 1,536 mg sodium, 4 g fiber

25 minutes

Serves 4

---

12 ounces fusilli

¾ cup frozen peas

1½ teaspoons grated
    lemon zest

3 tablespoons fresh
   lemon juice, plus
   more to taste (from
   about 2 lemons total)

¼ cup low-sodium
   chicken or vegetable
   broth

2 tablespoons chopped
   fresh mint, plus
   2 tablespoons thinly
   sliced mint

3 tablespoons finely
   chopped fresh Italian
   (flat-leaf) parsley

¼ cup finely chopped
   shallots

   Salt and freshly
   ground pepper
   to taste

¼ cup olive oil

1 6-ounce can
   oil-packed tuna,
   drained and broken
   into pieces

1 cup canned or freshly
   cooked chickpeas,
   drained

Pasta Salad with Tuna, Chickpeas & Lemon-Mint Dressing

Like the Summer Vegetable Pasta Salad (page 50), this dish takes less than 30 minutes to prepare but needs to be refrigerated for at least an hour before serving. It can also be "flash chilled" (see Tip, page 32). The moist oil-packed tuna clings to the noodles, the chickpeas add substance, and the green peas provide sweetness. The chicken broth in the lemony dressing reduces the amount of oil needed, and the mint helps bring the flavor up another notch. Serve over a bed of greens if you like.

Bring a large pot of salted water to a boil. Add the pasta and cook according to the package instructions until al dente, adding the peas during the last 5 minutes of cooking. Drain the pasta and peas, then rinse briefly to cool. (It's all right if the pasta is still a little warm, and it's best not to drown it in cold water.) Set aside in a colander to drain completely.

Meanwhile, combine the lemon zest, 3 tablespoons lemon juice, the broth, 2 tablespoons chopped mint, parsley, and shallots in a large bowl. Season with salt and pepper. Slowly drizzle in the olive oil, whisking constantly, to form an emulsified vinaigrette (see page 44).

Add the pasta and peas to the vinaigrette along with the tuna and chickpeas. Toss well, season with salt and pepper, and refrigerate for at least 1 hour or up to overnight.

Before serving, add more lemon juice, salt, and pepper, and stir in the sliced mint.

PER SERVING: 640 calories,
30 g protein, 86 g carbohydrate,
20 g fat (3 g saturated),
8 mg cholesterol, 423 mg sodium,
9 g fiber

25 minutes

Serves 4

SALAD

¼	cup sliced almonds
2	tablespoons sesame seeds
2	hearts of romaine, cut into 1-inch strips (or 10 ounces pre-cleaned, chopped romaine)
1	cup pre-washed baby spinach
1	cup pre-grated carrots
4	green onions, thinly sliced
1	pound precooked boneless, skinless chicken breasts, cut into 1- by 2-inch pieces
1½	cups bean sprouts
2 to 3	ounces daikon sprouts (optional)

DRESSING

¼	cup fresh orange juice (from about 1 orange)
2	tablespoons unseasoned rice vinegar
2	teaspoons soy sauce
½	teaspoon Asian sesame oil
2	tablespoons vegetable oil
	Salt and freshly ground

PER SERVING: 360 calories, 40 g protein, 12 g carbohydrate, 17 g fat (2 g saturated), 96 mg cholesterol, 260 mg sodium, 4 g fiber

Chinese Chicken Salad

This recipe, a twist on a classic, is a good way to use up leftover rotisserie chicken. It can be served on its own for a light meal. For bigger appetites, serve with pot stickers or sesame crackers.

To make the salad, preheat the oven or toaster oven to 400°F. Spread the almonds on a baking sheet and bake until golden, about 4 minutes. Transfer to a bowl to cool. Repeat with sesame seeds, toasting them about 2 minutes. Transfer to a bowl to cool.

Combine the romaine, spinach, carrots, green onions, chicken, bean sprouts, and daikon sprouts, if using, in a salad bowl. Add the cooled almonds.

To make the dressing, whisk together the orange juice, vinegar, and soy sauce in a bowl. Slowly drizzle in the sesame oil and vegetable oil, whisking constantly, to form an emulsified vinaigrette (see page 44). Add the sesame seeds and stir to combine.

Add the salad dressing to the salad, season with salt and pepper, and toss to combine. Serve at once.

NOTE: If your supermarket doesn't carry pre-grated carrots, simply grate some carrots yourself. Daikon sprouts, found in farmers' markets and gourmet supermarkets, are spicy, decorative sprouts that often are sold with the roots attached. The roots should be removed.

Rice Noodle Salad
with Chicken & Peanuts

Here's another salad that uses up leftover rotisserie chicken, one of the most versatile ingredients in the kitchen. Alternatively, use leftover roast pork loin or baked, marinated tofu. You can make this up to a day ahead, but wait to add the peanuts and watercress until right before serving.

Bring a large pot of water to a boil for the noodles. When the water is ready, cook the noodles for 2 to 3 minutes, or according to the package directions. Drain and rinse briefly to cool, then drain again, shaking the colander vigorously. Set aside to drain completely while you assemble the other ingredients.

Mix together the lime juice, vinegar, and fish sauce in a bowl. Add the sugar and stir until dissolved. Slowly drizzle in the peanut oil and sesame oil, whisking constantly, to form an emulsified vinaigrette (see page 44).

Combine the chicken, cucumber, green onions, and watercress in a bowl. Toss with about one-third of the dressing. Place the noodles in large bowl and drizzle with the remaining vinaigrette. Toss the noodles until they are evenly coated.

Distribute the noodles evenly among four plates, then top with the salad. Garnish each plate with the peanuts and serve.

25 minutes

Serves 4

- 8 ounces rice stick noodles (see Note, page 40), broken into large pieces
- ¼ cup fresh lime juice (from about 2 limes)
- 3 tablespoons unseasoned rice vinegar
- 2 tablespoons Asian fish sauce
- 1 tablespoon sugar
- 3 tablespoons peanut or vegetable oil
- 1 teaspoon Asian sesame oil
- 8 ounces precooked, boneless skinless chicken, cut into thin strips
- ½ English hothouse cucumber, sliced into half moons
- 6 green onions, thinly sliced
- 1 bunch watercress or arugula, thick stems removed
- ⅓ cup roasted and lightly salted peanuts, coarsely chopped

PER SERVING: 566 calories, 33 g protein, 56 g carbohydrate, 24 g fat (5 g saturated), 76 mg cholesterol, 849 mg sodium, 3 g fiber

2   tablespoons
     achiote paste

1   teaspoon
     ground cumin

1½   teaspoons salt,
     plus more to taste

¼   cup vegetable oil

4   boneless, skinless
     chicken half breasts,
     about 6 ounces each

⅛   teaspoon cayenne
     pepper, plus more
     to taste

1   teaspoon sugar

¼   cup fresh lime juice,
     plus more to taste
     (from about 2 limes)

1   bunch arugula or
     watercress

1   medium jicama (about
     1 pound), cut into strips

     Warm tortillas
     for serving

PER SERVING: 175 calories,
28 g protein, 11 g carbohydrate,
2 g fat (0 g saturated),
68 mg cholesterol, 84 mg sodium,
1 g fiber. The calories and other
nutrients absorbed from
marinades vary and are difficult
to estimate, so the marinade is
not included in this analysis.

Achiote Chicken with Jicama Salad

Widely used in Mexico's Yucatán region, achiote paste is made of ground annatto seeds, spices, vinegar, and sometimes garlic. Mixed with oil and additional seasonings, achiote makes an instant marinade that imparts an intense flavor and an appealing saffron-red color to meat and fish. In this recipe, chicken breasts are marinated in achiote, then quickly broiled. The chicken is placed on top of a salad of crisp jicama and arugula dressed with lime juice and a touch of cayenne. (See photo on page 45.)

Preheat the broiler, placing the rack about 4 inches from the heating element.

In a bowl, break up the achiote paste with a fork until powdery, then mix in the cumin, 1½ teaspoons salt, and the vegetable oil. Arrange the chicken breasts in a shallow dish and pour the achiote mixture on top, turning the chicken to coat it evenly. Set aside to marinate for at least 10 minutes and up to 2 hours.

Scrape off any large clumps of marinade from the chicken breasts. Place the breasts on a foil-lined baking sheet and broil until cooked through, 10 to 15 minutes, depending on their thickness. When done, remove the chicken from the oven, tent with foil, and set aside to rest.

Meanwhile, whisk together the cayenne pepper, sugar, lime juice, and salt to taste in a large bowl.

Trim off and discard the woody stems from the arugula and coarsely chop the leaves. Add the jicama and the arugula to the bowl with the dressing and toss to coat. The jicama should have a kick of cayenne and tart lime.

To serve, slice each chicken breast crosswise into 4 large pieces. Place the salad on a large platter and arrange the chicken pieces on top. Serve with warm tortillas.

> **NOTE:** You can find fresh jicama and bricks of achiote paste in Latin American markets and in supermarkets with large Hispanic sections. To prepare jicama, cut it in half, then stand each half on its flat end and trim off the skin with a sharp knife or vegetable peeler (if using a peeler, be sure to peel off any fibrous strings). Cut the halves into ¼-inch slices, then stack them and cut them again into long strips.

Grilled Chicken Salad
with Tomatoes & Mozzarella

30 minutes

Serves 4

Italy's insalata caprese is a fabulous combination of fresh mozzarella, tomatoes, basil, and olive oil that captures the flavor of summer. In this contemporary variation, it's best to use the ripest summer tomatoes and sweetest corn available. If you like, serve with thick slices of lightly oiled and grilled Italian bread.

3 ears fresh yellow corn, husked

4 boneless, skinless chicken half breasts, about 7 ounces each

Salt and freshly ground pepper to taste

1 pound vine-ripened tomatoes or 1 pint cherry tomatoes

2 large sprigs fresh basil

7 to 8 ounces good-quality fresh mozzarella

2 to 3 tablespoons extra virgin olive oil

Fresh lemon juice or champagne vinegar to taste

If you plan to use a grill, prepare a fire or preheat a gas grill for cooking over medium heat.

Bring a large pot of water to a boil and have ready a large bowl of ice water. Drop the corn into the boiling water and blanch until crisp-tender when pierced with a knife, 2 to 4 minutes, depending on the corn's ripeness and freshness. Drain the corn and immediately plunge the ears into the ice water until cool. Drain and set aside.

Meanwhile, season the chicken breasts on both sides with salt and pepper. Place the chicken breasts on the grill, or on a seasoned grill pan over high heat, and cook until the chicken is no longer pink in the middle, 5 to 7 minutes per side. Remove from the heat and let rest, tented with foil, for about 5 minutes.

While the chicken is cooking, cut the corn kernels off the cobs. If using vine-ripened tomatoes, cut into a dice just slightly larger than the corn kernels. If using cherry tomatoes, cut them in half. Remove the leaves from the basil sprigs and mince. Cut the mozzarella into a dice about the same size as the diced tomato.

Combine the corn, tomatoes, basil, and mozzarella in a large bowl. Add 2 tablespoons of the olive oil and season with salt and pepper. Toss gently and taste. Add more olive oil and/or a drizzle of lemon juice or vinegar if the salad needs a little boost of flavor.

Slice the grilled chicken breasts into strips and divide among four plates. Top each with a mound of the salad, including some of the juices. Serve at once.

[**NOTE:** Fresh mozzarella, which is sold packed in brine, is available in many supermarket delis and in cheese shops.]

TIP: An easy way to remove corn silk is to rub the husked corn with a clean towel. Instead of boiling, you can also steam the corn.

PER SERVING: 370 calories, 40 g protein, 17 g carbohydrate, 16 g fat (8 g saturated), 106 mg cholesterol, 279 mg sodium, 4 g fiber

25 minutes

Serves 4 to 6

GLAZED WALNUTS

¾	cup walnut pieces
1½	tablespoons maple syrup
	Pinch of curry powder
	Pinch of cayenne pepper
	Salt to taste

DRESSING

3	tablespoons vegetable oil
2½	teaspoons curry powder
⅔	cup nonfat plain yogurt
3	tablespoons fresh lemon juice (from about 1 lemon)
1½	teaspoons sugar
½	teaspoon salt
	Freshly ground black pepper to taste

SALAD

10	ounces boneless, skinless cooked turkey meat, cut into 1- by 2-inch strips (3 cups)
1	large tart-sweet apple such as Jonagold or McIntosh, cored and thinly sliced
2 to 3	stalks celery, thinly sliced
8	ounces mixed baby salad greens

PER SERVING: 278 calories, 18 g protein, 15 g carbohydrate, 10 g fat (2 g saturated), 36 mg cholesterol, 271 mg sodium, 3 g fiber

Turkey Salad with Creamy Curry Dressing

This light main course is fun to prepare in the days after Thanksgiving and other major turkey events, and it keeps the holiday mood going with flavors like spiced nuts and apples. You can buy spiced nuts, but they're easy to make. Just toss them in maple syrup and a pinch of cayenne and curry powder, then toast them in the oven. To streamline the preparation, start by preparing the glazed walnuts and the curry oil, and let them cool slightly while you chop the fresh ingredients.

Preheat the oven to 375°F. Cover a baking sheet with aluminum foil and lightly grease with vegetable oil.

To make the glazed walnuts, toss them in a bowl with the maple syrup, curry powder, cayenne, and salt. Taste one and make sure they are salty and spicy enough, and not overly sweet. Adjust the seasoning if necessary. Spread the walnuts on the prepared baking sheet and bake, checking occasionally, until the nuts are crisp and golden, 5 to 8 minutes. Let cool slightly, then remove from the pan.

To make the dressing, heat the oil in a small frying pan over low heat. Stir in the curry powder and sauté gently for 5 minutes. Scrape the curry oil into a large metal or heat-proof glass bowl (the curry oil can stain wooden bowls). When cool, whisk in the yogurt, lemon juice, sugar, salt, and pepper.

To assemble the salad, add the turkey, apple, celery, salad greens, and glazed walnuts to the bowl with the dressing. Season with salt and pepper. Toss to combine and serve.

TIP: Sautéing the curry powder in oil will prevent the dressing from having a raw, powdery taste.

35 minutes

Serves 4

- 10 ounces pre-washed baby spinach
- 2 large eggs
- 4 medium portobello mushrooms, cleaned and stems and gills removed

  Salt and freshly ground black pepper to taste
- 4 slices thick-cut bacon
- ¼ cup apple cider vinegar or raspberry vinegar
- ¼ cup olive oil

  Croutons

Spinach Salad with Roasted Portobello Mushrooms & Bacon

This twist on a classic spinach salad contains roasted portobellos instead of slivered button mushrooms, which elevates it from a side dish to a main course. It calls for several cooking methods—roasting, boiling, and sautéing—but it can all be done quickly if you don't mind multitasking.

Preheat the oven to 450°F. Place the spinach in a large salad bowl.

Place the eggs in a small saucepan and add water to cover by 1 inch. Bring to a rolling boil and cook for 8 minutes. Remove from the heat, drain, and let cool under running water for a few minutes. Peel and slice the eggs widthwise.

Meanwhile, place the mushrooms on a baking sheet, stem side up, sprinkle with salt and pepper, and roast until the mushrooms are very soft, 20 to 25 minutes. When they are done, cut into slices about ½ inch thick.

While the mushrooms are roasting, dice the bacon. Heat a sauté pan over medium heat and add the bacon. Brown, stirring occasionally, until crisp, about 8-10 minutes. Remove the bacon from the pan with a slotted spoon and place on paper towels to drain.

Drain most of the fat from the pan, then add the vinegar, oil, salt, and pepper. Heat gently until just heated through, then pour the mixture over the spinach, tossing quickly so the leaves wilt just slightly.

Add the bacon and croutons to the salad, season with salt and pepper, and toss to combine. Place on serving plates, top each salad with the egg and mushroom slices, and serve at once.

PER SERVING: 249 calories, 12 g protein, 9 g carbohydrate, 20 g fat (4 g saturated), 111 mg cholesterol, 207 mg sodium, 7 g fiber

TIP: In this recipe, removing the black gills from the underside of portobello mushrooms is a nice touch; otherwise the cooked mushrooms leak unsightly black juice into the salad. First pop off the stems, then gently scrape the gills off with a large soup spoon.

Grilled Steak Salad with Spring Onions & Arugula

In this recipe, the browned onions and warm steak soften the blue cheese and lightly wilt the arugula, which is dressed with sherry vinegar and walnut oil. Although green onions work fine, the spring onions that are sold at farmers' markets in season are a nice touch. The incredible sweetness of these baby onions, which look like leeks with a white or red bulbous end, is released when they are caramelized in a grill pan.

If you plan to use a grill, prepare a fire or preheat a gas grill for cooking over medium-high heat.

Rub the steak with the garlic and season liberally on both sides with salt and pepper. Place the steak in the middle of a preheated grill pan or on the grill and cook to the desired doneness, 5 to 6 minutes on each side for medium-rare. When the steak is done, remove it from the heat and let rest, tented with foil, for at least 5 minutes.

While the steak cooks, whisk together the vinegar and mustard in a small bowl; season with salt and pepper. Slowly drizzle in the oil, whisking constantly, to form an emulsified vinaigrette (see page 44).

After removing the steak from the heat, add the onions to the pan or the grill and let brown undisturbed for 1 minute. Turn over and brown on the second side for 1 minute. Remove the onions from the heat and slice.

Combine the onions and arugula in a bowl and add just enough of the dressing to coat the leaves; there may be extra dressing. Toss to coat. Season the salad with salt and pepper, toss again, and divide the salad among four serving plates.

Slice the steak thinly against the grain. Divide the steak on top of the salad, fanning out the slices, sprinkle the blue cheese on top, and serve at once.

25 minutes

Serves 4

1	pound flank steak
2	cloves garlic, minced
	Salt and freshly ground pepper to taste
2	tablespoons sherry vinegar
1/4	teaspoon Dijon mustard
1/4	cup walnut, hazelnut, or extra virgin olive oil
2	large spring onions or 6 green onions
8 to 10	cups loose baby arugula leaves, or leaves from about 1 1/2 bunches arugula
1/3	cup crumbled blue cheese

TIP: If you use arugula bunches rather than loose leaves, discard the thick stems, then cut the leaves in half.

PER SERVING: 365 calories, 28 g protein, 5 g carbohydrate, 26 g fat (8 g saturated), 67 mg cholesterol, 252 mg sodium, 1 g fiber

Pasta

A well-crafted plate of pasta is one of my favorite meals. It's a perfect solution for working cooks since a great sauce can be made in the time it takes to boil a pot of water and cook some spaghetti.

One of my most memorable assignments at *The San Francisco Chronicle* was when my colleague Lesli Neilson and I visited more than forty restaurants in a search for the best pasta in North Beach, San Francisco's Little Italy.

After sharing and rating eighty-two plates of noodles, Lesli and I still weren't sick of pasta, despite a few bad experiences with undercooked clams and clumpy, cream-laden sauces. Though we ate plenty of excellent restaurant pastas, we realized that we both prefer to make it at home, just the way we like it.

The following are our cardinal rules for cooking the perfect plate of pasta:

• First bring 4 quarts of water seasoned with 2 teaspoons salt to a boil (there's no need to add oil to the water). Using plenty of water will help the pasta cook evenly, and salting the water well is essential: it gives the pasta some flavor of its own, which helps bring the dish together—especially in the case of pastas served with simple sauces.

• Add the pasta to the water only after it has come to a full rolling boil. Stir the pasta after adding it to the water and frequently thereafter.

• Perfectly al dente, or "to the tooth," pasta isn't crunchy, nor is it soft. Instead, it should be satisfyingly chewy. If the center is slightly lighter in color than the rest of the pasta when it's bitten into, it's not quite cooked through; give it another minute or two.

• If the recipe requires it, reserve some pasta water for the sauce. Not only does the water thin some sauces to the right consistency, but the gluten from the pasta adds body to the sauce.

• Drain pasta well—watery pasta can ruin a good sauce—but don't rinse it, as this will wash away the starch that helps the sauce cling to the pasta.

• Rather than simply topping a bowl of pasta with a pool of sauce, stir the pasta into the warm sauce to better marry the two.

Facing page: Penne with Radicchio, Pancetta & Pecans (recipe on page 81); Spaghetti alla Carbonara with Peas (recipe on page 79)

20 minutes

Serves 4

1½ pounds broccoli crowns

¼ cup pine nuts

12 ounces orecchiette

¼ cup extra virgin olive oil

1 to 2 pinches red pepper flakes

4 cloves garlic, minced

Salt and freshly ground pepper to taste

Pecorino cheese to taste

Orecchiette with Broccoli

In this recipe, the broccoli is cooked at the same time as the pasta, then both are sautéed in olive oil, garlic, and red pepper flakes for an extra punch of flavor. Orecchiette ("little ears"), so named because of its cupped shape, holds the light sauce perfectly. It is becoming more widely available, but if you can't find it, substitute medium pasta shells.

Fill a pot with salted water (see page 65), cover, and bring to a boil.

Cut the broccoli into pieces slightly larger than the uncooked pasta. Either discard the stems or peel and cut into small cubes.

Place the pine nuts in a small, heavy frying pan and toast over medium heat, stirring often, until lightly browned, 3 to 5 minutes.

When the water reaches a boil, add the pasta and cook over high heat, stirring constantly to keep the pasta from sticking, for 1 minute. Add the broccoli and return to a boil. Reduce the heat to medium and cook, stirring often, until the pasta is al dente and the broccoli is very tender. Remove and reserve ¾ cup of the cooking water. Drain the pasta and broccoli.

When the pasta is almost done, heat the olive oil over medium-low heat in a sauté pan that will fit the pasta and broccoli. Add the red pepper flakes and garlic and sauté until the garlic just begins to release its aroma, about 1 minute. Remove the pan from the heat before the garlic begins to brown.

Add the drained pasta and broccoli to the skillet. Stir over low heat for 1 minute to combine. Stir in enough of the pasta water to form a light sauce, season with salt and pepper, and stir in the pine nuts.

To serve, divide the pasta among four bowls and top each serving with plenty of cheese.

TIP: The traditional version of this Southern Italian recipe features broccoli rabe (also called rapini), a pleasantly bitter, delicately flavored cousin of broccoli. If you find it in your grocery store or farmers' market, blanch it in the water until tender, about 3 minutes, and remove it before adding the pasta to the water. Drain the broccoli rabe and let it cool briefly. Chop it coarsely and add it to the pan after you sauté the garlic, then season with salt and sauté for a few minutes before proceeding with the rest of the recipe as directed.

PER SERVING: 571 calories, 18 g protein, 81 g carbohydrate, 21 g fat (3 g saturated), 0 mg cholesterol, 55 mg sodium, 9 g fiber

Pasta e Fagioli

Meaning simply "pasta and beans," pasta e fagioli is a traditional Italian dish that is meant to be soft and soupy. If you like, you can use up odds and ends of different kinds of short pasta.

Fill a pot with salted water (see page 65), cover, and bring to a boil. When the water reaches a boil, add the pasta and cook, stirring often, until it is a few minutes past al dente, soft but not mushy. Drain, reserving about 2 cups of the cooking water.

While the pasta cooks, heat the oil in a sauté pan over low heat. Add the garlic, rosemary, and the red pepper flakes and cook until the garlic is just golden and fragrant, about 1 minute. Add the tomatoes and simmer gently for about 5 minutes.

Add the drained beans and their reserved liquid and some salt and pepper to the pan, then bring to a simmer. Simmer for 5 to 8 minutes, stirring occasionally and crushing about half of the beans with the back of a wooden spoon.

Return the drained pasta to the large pot and add the beans and enough of the reserved pasta water to make the dish nice and soupy. Bring to a boil, then remove from the heat, cover, and let sit for 5 minutes. Serve in shallow bowls with a drizzle of olive oil and more red pepper flakes to taste.

30 minutes
Serves 4

- 8 ounces medium pasta shells or other cup-shaped or short pasta
- 1/4 cup extra virgin olive oil, plus more for drizzling
- 3 cloves garlic, finely chopped
- 1 large sprig fresh rosemary, needles finely chopped

  Pinch of red pepper flakes, plus more to taste
- 1/2 cup chopped or pureed fresh or canned tomatoes
- 2 15-ounce cans cannellini or Great Northern beans, or 3 1/3 cups cooked beans, 1/2 cup of their liquid reserved

  Salt and freshly ground black pepper to taste

PER SERVING: 471 calories, 17 g protein, 73 g carbohydrate, 16 g fat (2 g saturated), 0 mg cholesterol, 569 mg sodium, 11 g fiber

40 minutes

Serves 4 to 5

½ head savoy cabbage
or other small
green cabbage

4 medium red potatoes

8 ounces pizzoccheri
or whole-wheat
or spinach fettuccine

¼ cup extra virgin
olive oil

6 fresh sage leaves

Salt and freshly
ground pepper
to taste

4 ounces fontina
cheese, cut into
bite-size pieces

2 to 4 tablespoons
freshly grated
Parmesan cheese

PER SERVING: 408 calories,
15 g protein, 46 g carbohydrate,
19 g fat (5 g saturated),
22 mg cholesterol,
185 mg sodium, 9 g fiber

Pizzoccheri

Italy offers obscure pastas from regions far and wide, so many that it could take a culinary lifetime to explore them all. Pizzoccheri, a baked noodle dish from an Alpine valley near the Swiss border, is one of them. This potato- and cabbage-filled dish, topped with fontina cheese and browned in the oven, is wonderful in winter. If you can't find pizzoccheri, the dish's traditional buckwheat noodles, at an Italian deli, use whole-wheat or spinach ribbon noodles instead, though they don't have quite the same hearty texture and unique, earthy flavor as the original.

Preheat the broiler, placing the rack about 4 inches from the heating element. Grease a 13- by 9-inch baking dish. Fill two large pots with salted water (see page 65), cover, and bring both to a boil.

Core the cabbage and slice it into ribbons the same width as the noodles. Halve the potatoes, then slice them into rounds about ¼ inch thick.

When the water reaches a boil, add the cabbage and potatoes to one of the pots, return to a low boil, and cook until the potatoes are tender but firm, 8 to 10 minutes. Drain and set aside.

Meanwhile, in the other pot, cook the noodles according to the package directions until al dente. Drain and set aside.

Heat the olive oil in a small frying pan. Add the sage leaves and fry until slightly browned, about 1 minute. Remove the leaves from the oil and set aside.

Combine the drained pasta and vegetables in one of the pots. Stir in the sage oil and season with salt and pepper. Transfer the mixture to the prepared baking dish, dot with the fontina and sage leaves, and sprinkle evenly with the Parmesan. Broil until lightly golden and the cheese is melted, 5 to 10 minutes. Serve at once.

TIP: Be sure to add a generous amount of salt to the cooking water for the pasta and the vegetables, because it's difficult to add salt to these dense, starchy ingredients later.

Penne with Roasted Eggplant & Pesto

Pasta with fresh pesto is hard to resist. The roasted eggplant and tomatoes in this version aren't traditional, but they provide some substance and contrast to the rich noodles, making it suitable as an entree rather than a first-course pasta. To cut down on fat, this version has less olive oil than most, but I compensate by adding a little pasta cooking water to thin the sauce.

Preheat the oven to 375°F.

Fill a pot with salted water (see page 65), cover, and bring to a boil. Cook the pasta according to the package directions. Drain the pasta, reserving ½ cup of the cooking water.

While the pasta is cooking, slice the eggplant into rounds ⅛ inch thick. Grease a baking sheet with vegetable oil, then arrange the eggplant slices on the baking sheet in a single layer. Sprinkle with salt and roast for 10 minutes, until lightly browned on the bottom. Flip over and continue cooking until completely tender, another 10 minutes. Let cool, then cut into strips 1 inch thick.

Place the pine nuts, garlic, and ¼ teaspoon salt in the bowl of a food processor. Pulse until finely pureed and crumbly but not oily. Add the basil and cheese and pulse until pureed. Add the olive oil in a thin stream while pureeing. Taste and adjust the amount of salt, if necessary.

After draining the pasta, return it to its pot with the eggplant and the pesto. Add the pasta cooking water a few tablespoons at a time just until the pesto forms a creamy sauce that clings to the pasta. Add the tomatoes and salt to taste and toss to combine.

To serve, divide the pasta among three or four bowls, garnish each bowl with a basil leaf, and pass the Parmesan cheese at the table.

[**NOTE:** I call for penne rigate—meaning penne with ridges—because it integrates with other ingredients better than smooth penne.]

TIP: When I go to the trouble of getting out my food processor, I like to make a double batch of pesto and save some for later. When refrigerating leftover pesto, cover it completely with oil to prevent the basil from oxidizing and turning an off color. Allow it to return to room temperature while you make the pasta. If you're going to freeze pesto, omit the cheese. Place the pesto in a small, freezer-safe resealable bag and allow the bag to lie flat in the freezer. Defrost the pesto at room temperature for 1 to 2 hours, then stir in the cheese before using.

---

35 minutes

Serves 3 to 4

- 12 ounces penne rigate
- 8 ounces Japanese or globe eggplant
  - Vegetable oil for the pan
- ¼ teaspoon salt, plus more to taste
- ⅓ cup pine nuts
- 1 clove garlic, peeled and trimmed
- 2 cups fresh basil leaves (from about 5 large sprigs), plus a few more leaves for garnish
- ¼ cup grated Parmesan cheese plus more for serving
- ¼ cup extra virgin olive oil
- ½ pint cherry tomatoes, halved, or 6 oil-packed sun-dried tomatoes, drained and thinly sliced

PER SERVING: 533 calories, 15 g protein, 63 g carbohydrate, 25 g fat (5 g saturated), 4 mg cholesterol, 244 mg sodium, 6 g fiber

30 minutes

Serves 6

1 pound linguine

1 tablespoon extra virgin olive oil

4 cloves garlic, minced

1½ pounds rock shrimp or peeled and deveined medium shrimp

10 fresh basil leaves, coarsely chopped, plus more leaves for garnish

1 tablespoon minced orange zest

1 cup dry vermouth

½ cup low-sodium chicken broth

Juice of 1 lemon

½ cup light or regular whipping cream

2 tablespoons unsalted butter

Salt and freshly ground pepper to taste

Linguine with Vermouth & Orange-Scented Shrimp

This dish pairs intriguing sweet and savory flavors. Fresh basil and orange zest brighten the sweet rock shrimp, and the rich, creamy pasta sauce gets a kick from vermouth and lemon juice.

Fill a pot with salted water (see page 65), cover, and bring to a boil. Cook the pasta according to the package directions. Drain the pasta, reserving ½ cup of the cooking water.

While the pasta is cooking, heat the olive oil in a sauté pan over medium heat. Add the garlic and cook for 1 minute. Add the shrimp, basil, and orange zest and cook just until the shrimp turn pink, turning the shrimp once, about 2 minutes total. Remove the shrimp mixture from the pan and keep warm.

Add the vermouth, chicken broth, and lemon juice and deglaze the pan, stirring to scrape up any bits that may have stuck to the bottom. Increase the heat to high and cook until the liquid is reduced by about a third, about 5 minutes. Reduce the heat to low, stir in the cream, and simmer gently until thickened, about 2 minutes. Whisk in the butter and season the sauce with salt and pepper.

Return the shrimp to the pan, then add the pasta and stir over low heat until incorporated, about 1 minute. Add a little bit of the reserved pasta water to thin the sauce, if necessary. Serve in pasta bowls and garnish each serving with basil leaves.

PER SERVING: 578 calories, 26 g protein, 52 g carbohydrate, 13 g fat (5 g saturated), 185 mg cholesterol, 335 mg sodium, 2 g fiber

40 minutes

Serves 4 to 6

1   large bunch winter
    greens, such as
    Swiss chard or kale

1   pound fusilli or
    corkscrew pasta

¼   cup extra virgin
    olive oil

    Pinch of red pepper
    flakes

½   sweet Maui or yellow
    onion, thinly sliced

½   cup golden or dark
    raisins

2   cloves garlic,
    thinly sliced

⅓   cup slivered almonds

    Crushed garlic
    croutons and/or
    grated Parmesan
    cheese

PER SERVING: 480 calories,
14 g protein, 75 g carbohydrate,
15 g fat (2 g saturated),
0 mg cholesterol,
360 mg sodium, 6 g fiber

Fusilli with Winter Greens, Onions & Raisins

In this vegetarian dish, a handful of plumped raisins offsets the slightly bitter Swiss chard or kale, and toasted almonds add a nice crunch. Because the dish is so simple, it's important to season the cooking water very well. You first cook the greens in the water, then add the pasta, which allows the pasta to absorb some of the flavor of the greens. Later, after the pasta has cooked and released some of its gluten into the water, some of this rich liquid goes right into the sauce, adding moisture, flavor, and a little body.

Fill a pot with salted water (see page 65), cover, and bring to a boil.

Stack the greens and trim the stems slightly, then slice the leaves and stems into ¼-inch strips. Cut these strips into 2-inch lengths so they resemble shape of the pasta (if you slice them too thinly they'll clump up in the sauce).

When the water reaches a boil, add the greens. Return the water to a simmer and cook until the stems are tender, 5 to 8 minutes for chard and 10 to 12 minutes for kale. Drain the greens in a colander over a large bowl, reserving the cooking water.

Return the cooking water to the pot and bring to a boil again. Add the pasta and cook according to the package directions. Drain the pasta, reserving 1 cup of the cooking water.

While the greens and pasta are cooking, heat the olive oil in a sauté pan over medium heat, then add the red pepper flakes. Stir for a moment or two, then add the onion. Cook until lightly browned, about 5 minutes. Add the raisins, reduce the heat slightly, and cook until the onion is tender, about 5 minutes. Add the garlic and stir for another minute. Set aside.

Put the almonds in a small frying pan over medium heat and toast, tossing them occasionally, until they're brown and fragrant, 5 to 8 minutes. Watch carefully, as they burn easily. Transfer the almonds to a plate and let cool.

When the pasta is almost done, add the greens to the onion mixture with ½ cup of the pasta cooking water. Stir and heat gently for a few minutes. Season with salt.

Add the pasta to the pan and stir to combine. If you need a little more liquid, add the remaining ½ cup of the cooking water. To serve, place in bowls and top each serving with almonds and croutons and/or Parmesan cheese.

TIP: To streamline the preparation, begin cooking the pasta and greens before you slice the garlic and onions.

Fusilli with Tuna, Capers & Chickpeas

As many a harried Italian mother knows, a wonderful tasting and protein-rich pasta sauce can be made from a can—several cans, that is, of tuna, chickpeas, and tomatoes. Of course, using the best-quality ingredients makes this dish even better. Regular water-packed tuna works fine, but tuna packed in olive oil is even better.

Fill a pot with salted water (see page 65), cover, and bring to a boil. Cook the pasta according to the package directions. Drain.

While the pasta cooks, heat the olive oil in a large sauté pan over medium heat. Add the red pepper flakes and sauté for 30 seconds. Add the onion and sauté until softened, about 10 minutes.

Add the tuna to the pan, breaking it into bite-size pieces with a wooden spoon. Add the chickpeas, tomatoes, salt, and pepper and stir. Bring to a simmer and cook, stirring occasionally, for 10 to 15 minutes.

Add the capers to the sauce. Taste and adjust the amount of salt and pepper, if necessary. Add the pasta to sauce. Stir briefly over low heat, taste, and add more salt if necessary. Serve in shallow bowls.

30 minutes

Serves 4 to 6

- 1 pound fusilli
- 2 tablespoons olive oil
- 1/4 teaspoon red pepper flakes
- 1/2 onion, diced
- 1 6-ounce can oil-packed tuna, drained
- 1 15-ounce can chickpeas, drained and rinsed
- 1 14 1/2 -ounce can chopped tomatoes

  Salt and freshly ground pepper to taste
- 1 tablespoon drained capers, coarsely chopped

PER SERVING: 410 calories, 19 g protein, 62 g carbohydrate, 9 g fat (1 g saturated), 9 mg cholesterol, 391 mg sodium, 6 g fiber

Linguine with Puttanesca Sauce

30 minutes

Serves 4 to 6

1 pound linguine
2 to 4 tablespoons extra virgin olive oil
½ teaspoon red pepper flakes
½ teaspoon dried oregano
6 cloves garlic, thinly sliced
5 small anchovy fillets
1 28-ounce can chopped tomatoes, with half of the juices reserved
½ cup dry-cured black olives, pitted and coarsely chopped
2 tablespoons small capers, drained
Freshly ground pepper to taste
⅓ cup finely chopped fresh Italian (flat-leaf) parsley

Puttanesca sauce may well be the original working cook recipe, since it may have been created for the world's oldest profession. According to one story, it got the name puttanesca, which means "of the harlot," because working girls could prepare it quickly between engagements. Whatever the origins of the name, it seems appropriate for this spicy, zesty sauce. Served with linguine, it makes a very easy meal, especially since the only fresh ingredient is parsley; everything else comes straight out of the pantry.

Fill a pot with salted water (see page 65), cover, and bring to a boil. Cook the pasta according to the package directions.

While the pasta is cooking, heat the olive oil in a large sauté pan over medium-low heat. Add the red pepper flakes, oregano, and garlic and sauté until the garlic is just golden, about 1 minute. Add the anchovy fillets and mash with a spoon until they dissolve into the other ingredients. Add the tomatoes and their juice, the olives, and capers to the sauce, plus a grinding of black pepper. Increase heat to bring to a simmer, then simmer steadily for about 7 minutes. Taste and add more salt and pepper if needed.

Drain the pasta and add it to the sauce. Warm over low heat, stirring, for 1 minute. Add most of the parsley to the pasta and stir. To serve, divide among shallow bowls and sprinkle the remaining parsley over each serving.

PER SERVING: 328 calories, 11 g protein, 51 g carbohydrate, 11 g fat (1 g saturated), 3 mg cholesterol, 803 mg sodium, 4 g fiber

TIP: You can make this sauce up to a day or two ahead; just chop and add the parsley the day you serve it. You also can play around with the amount of olive oil. Traditional recipes contain a lot of it because it adds flavor and body.

Spaghetti & Meatballs

To make quick work of preparing meatballs, this recipe relies on prepared meat-loaf mix, a combination of fresh ground meats and seasonings found in many grocery store meat departments. You roll the raw mix into balls that cook under the broiler in less than 10 minutes. The accompanying marinara sauce takes just five minutes to put together and simmers while you make the meatballs.

Preheat the broiler, placing the rack about 4 inches from the heating element.

Fill a pot with salted water (see page 65), cover, and bring to a boil. Cook the spaghetti according to the package directions.

Meanwhile, heat the olive oil in a large sauté pan over medium-low heat, then add the garlic, red pepper flakes, and oregano. Cook until the garlic becomes fragrant, about 1 minute, then add the tomatoes. Increase the heat to bring to a simmer and cook for 10 minutes. Remove the garlic.

While the sauce is simmering, roll the meat-loaf mix into 20 to 24 meatballs, each about the size of a walnut, and place on a baking sheet. Broil the meatballs for about 4 minutes. Turn the meatballs over and continue broiling until cooked through, about 4 minutes more.

When the spaghetti is done, drain it, then add it to the sauce in the pan and toss to coat. To serve, divide the spaghetti among four serving bowls and top each with an equal number of meatballs, some Parmesan, and the basil leaves, if using.

NOTE: Many meat-loaf mixes tend to be high in fat and sodium. If this is an issue for you, use only 12 ounces of the mix.

30 minutes

Serves 4

- 12 ounces spaghetti
- 2 tablespoons extra virgin olive oil
- 3 cloves garlic, peeled and lightly crushed
- Pinch of red pepper flakes
- Pinch of dried oregano
- 1 28-ounce can chopped tomatoes
- 12 ounces to 1 pound raw meat-loaf mix
- Grated Parmesan cheese for serving
- Torn fresh basil leaves for serving (optional)

PER SERVING: 654 calories, 26 g protein, 81 g carbohydrate, 26 g fat (8 g saturated), 40 mg cholesterol, 517 g sodium, 10 g fiber

30 minutes

Serves 4 to 6

2½ to 3   pounds small live
          clams, well scrubbed

2   tablespoons
          cornmeal

2   teaspoons
          vegetable or olive
          oil

1   onion, chopped

7   ounces meat
          or poultry chorizo,
          chopped or
          crumbled

1   pound fettuccine

1   14½-ounce can
          chopped tomatoes

¼   cup chopped
          fresh Italian
          (flat-leaf) parsley

          Salt as needed

Fettuccine with Clams & Chorizo

Clams and smoky sausages are an ideal pairing. In Spain, you might find them nestled together in a fluffy paella; in Portugal, clams and linguiça are steamed with white wine, tomatoes, and parsley in a dish called amêijoas na Cataplana. The following recipe features this simple combination, which requires very few other ingredients for great flavor.

Fill a pot with salted water (see page 65), cover, and bring to a boil.

Place the clams in a bowl. Cover them with water and sprinkle in the cornmeal. Set aside.

Heat the oil in a Dutch oven. Add the onion and sauté until translucent, about 5 minutes. Add the chorizo and cook, stirring often, until just browned, 2 minutes.

Add the pasta to the boiling water and start cooking according to the package instructions.

Add the tomatoes with their liquid to the chorizo. Simmer until the liquid is slightly reduced, 5 minutes.

Lift the clams out of their soaking water and rinse under cool running water. Add them to the chorizo with ½ cup fresh water. Bring to a simmer, stir, then cover and steam until the clams open and their flesh is no longer translucent, 7 or 8 minutes. Discard any clams that don't open.

Drain the pasta and stir it into the pot with the clams. Stir in most of the parsley and season with salt, if necessary.

To serve, ladle into pasta bowls and sprinkle the remaining parsley on top.

PER SERVING: 632 calories, 58 g protein, 56 g carbohydrate, 19 g fat (6 g saturated), 137 mg cholesterol, 849 mg sodium, 3 g fiber

TIP: Adding cornmeal to the clam-soaking water encourages the bivalves to open up and release any sand trapped in their shells. After soaking, lift the clams out of the water so that any sand left in the bottom of the bowl stays behind.

8	ounces rotini or other short spiral-shaped pasta
6	ounces green beans, trimmed and cut into 1-inch lengths
¼	cup natural chunky or smooth peanut butter
3	tablespoons orange juice
1	tablespoon regular or reduced-sodium soy sauce, plus more to taste
1	tablespoon unseasoned rice vinegar
8	ounces boneless, skinless chicken breasts, diced
	Salt to taste
1 to 2	teaspoons vegetable oil
½	red bell pepper, diced
	Sesame seeds for garnish
	Thinly sliced green onions for garnish

Peanut Butter Noodles with Chicken

Inspired by a Thai-style peanut sauce but without the usual chiles and other traditional spices, this pasta will appeal to both children and adults. The noodles are great warm or served at room temperature, and the velvety peanut sauce might be a good way to get your children to eat the chicken and vegetables that are tossed in. In this case, it's OK to rinse the pasta to cool it down because you'll have no problem making the thick sauce cling to it.

Fill a pot with salted water (see page 65), cover, and bring to a boil. Cook the pasta according to the package directions. About 8 minutes before the pasta is done, add the green beans to the pot. Increase the heat to high and return the water to a boil. Cook until the pasta and beans are done. Drain together, rinse briefly with cold water, and set aside.

While the pasta is cooking, place the peanut butter in a small bowl. Whisk in the orange juice, 2 tablespoons water, soy sauce, and vinegar. If using unsalted peanut butter, you may want to add an additional teaspoon of soy sauce.

Sprinkle the diced chicken evenly with salt. Heat the oil in a nonstick wok or frying pan over high heat and stir-fry the chicken until it is white on all sides, 4-5 minutes. Add the bell pepper, stir a few times, cover, reduce the heat to medium-low, and cook a few more minutes until the chicken is cooked through and the bell pepper is tender. Remove from the heat.

Add the pasta, green beans, and sauce to the chicken and toss until well combined. Taste and season with salt, if necessary.

Serve warm or at room temperature, each serving garnished with sesame seeds and green onions.

PER SERVING: 374 calories, 24 g protein, 46 g carbohydrates, 11 g fat (2 g saturated), 33 mg cholesterol, 252 mg sodium, 4 g fiber

TIP: Leave out the green beans or the bell pepper if your children don't like them, substituting vegetables they like better such as frozen peas or carrots. Just cook the frozen vegetables with the pasta as you do the green beans, following the package directions for cooking times.

Spaghetti alla Carbonara with Peas

In this classic dish, egg yolks form the base of a thin sauce. A bit of grated Parmesan and pecorino and some pancetta complement the fresh egg flavor, and peas add sweetness and a dash of green. (See photo on page 65.)

Fill a pot with salted water (see page 65), cover, and bring to a boil. Cook the pasta according to the package directions. About 5 minutes before the pasta is done, add the peas to the pasta water.

While the pasta is cooking, beat the egg yolks well in a large bowl. Stir in the cream, Parmesan, pecorino, and several grindings of pepper.

Sauté the pancetta in a frying pan over medium heat until just crisp, about 5-8 minutes. Drain on paper towels, then crumble or chop coarsely.

When the pasta and peas are done, drain, reserving ½ cup of the cooking water, and immediately add the pasta and peas to the bowl with the egg mixture. Top with the pancetta and toss everything together quickly so the eggs heat through but do not cook. Stir in ¼ cup of the reserved pasta water, or as much as needed to lightly moisten the sauce. Season with salt and pepper.

To serve, divide among shallow bowls and garnish with additional Parmesan, pecorino, and pepper.

[**NOTE:** According to some studies, uncooked eggs may not be safe, especially for those with compromised immune systems, since in rare instances they may carry salmonella.]

TIP: For a dish this simple, seasoning is important. Season the pasta water well, and use plenty of freshly ground pepper.

30 minutes
Serves 4

- 12 ounces spaghetti
- ½ cup frozen peas, or 8 ounces English peas, shelled
- 4 large egg yolks, at room temperature
- ¼ cup light or regular whipping cream
- 3 tablespoons grated Parmesan cheese, plus more for garnish
- 3 tablespoons grated pecorino cheese, plus more for garnish
- Freshly ground pepper to taste
- 3 ounces thinly sliced pancetta
- Salt to taste

PER SERVING: 534 calories, 29 g protein, 61 g carbohydrate, 19 g fat (7 g saturated), 243 mg cholesterol, 575 mg sodium, 3 g fiber

40 minutes

Serves 4

- 12 ounces gnocchi pasta or medium shells
- 12 ounces frozen quartered artichoke hearts
- 1 to 2 teaspoons olive oil
- 12 ounces spicy Italian sausage, removed from their casing and coarsely chopped
- ½ red onion, chopped
- 2 small red bell peppers, cut into 2-inch strips
- ¼ teaspoon red pepper flakes
- ¾ cup dry white wine
- 3 to 4 teaspoons fresh lemon juice (about a half lemon)
- ½ cup pre-grated Parmesan cheese, plus more for serving

  Salt and freshly ground black pepper to taste

Gnocchi Pasta with Artichokes & Italian Sausage

Shell-shaped gnocchi pasta resembles the more familiar Italian dumplings called gnocchi and catches thinner pasta sauces nicely. Italian sausage and delicate artichokes are a delicious combination, and white wine and lemon juice add a wonderful zip to the sauce.

Fill a pot with salted water (see page 65), cover, and bring to a boil. Cook the pasta according to the package directions. Drain the pasta, reserving about 1 cup of the cooking water.

While the pasta is cooking, prepare the artichoke hearts according to package directions. After defrosting, if the artichoke hearts are in large pieces, cut them in half through the core so that they are roughly the same size as the bell pepper pieces.

Heat the oil in a large sauté pan over medium-high heat and then add the sausage. Let brown for a minute or two per side, then use a spatula to break it up into smaller pieces. Remove the sausage from the pan and discard all but 1 to 2 tablespoons of the oil.

Add the onion to the oil remaining in the pan and sauté until translucent, about 5 minutes, then add the bell peppers and red pepper flakes to the pan and sauté, stirring frequently, 5 minutes more. Add the wine and deglaze the pan, stirring to scrape up any browned bits on the bottom of the pan. Bring to a low boil and cook until the wine is reduced by about half, 3 to 5 minutes.

Stir in the lemon juice, sausage, and artichokes and heat through. Reduce the heat to low and stir in the pasta and Parmesan and just enough of the pasta cooking water so that the sauce coats the pasta evenly. Continue to warm for about 1 minute to meld the flavors. Season well with salt and pepper. Serve in shallow bowls, passing additional Parmesan cheese at the table.

TIP: Use frozen plain artichoke hearts rather than jarred marinated artichoke hearts, which are too strongly flavored for this dish. You also can use fresh artichokes if you have an extra 20 minutes or so. Peel eight medium artichokes down to the delicate light green leaves and remove the prickly inner leaves, choke, and stems. Slice the remaining hearts and tender leaves into ¼-inch pieces. Blanch them in boiling, salted water with a few slices of lemon until they're tender, about 5 minutes, then use as directed.

PER SERVING: 616 calories, 27 g protein, 81 g carbohydrate, 17 g fat (6 g saturated), 41 mg cholesterol, 615 mg sodium, 8 g fiber

Penne with Radicchio, Pancetta & Pecans

Though they might notice bright red radicchio in salad mixes, many people aren't sure how to cook it. In this recipe, its bitterness is balanced by sweet balsamic vinegar, salty pancetta, crunchy pecans, and a dash of cream. A bit of sugar also helps take the edge off this trendy purple plant in the chicory family, but you may want to adjust the amount depending on the quality of your balsamic vinegar. The longer the balsamic has been aged, the more intensely flavored and sweet it will be. (See photo on page 64.)

Fill a pot with salted water (see page 65), cover, and bring to a boil. Cook the pasta according to the package directions. Drain, reserving ½ cup of the cooking water.

While the pasta is cooking, heat the olive oil in a large sauté pan over medium heat, then add the onion. Sauté until translucent, 5 minutes, then add the pancetta to the pan and continue sautéing, stirring occasionally, until the onion is tender and the pancetta is slightly crisp, about 5 minutes more.

Meanwhile, quarter the radicchio through the core, then trim off the bit of core from each wedge with diagonal cuts. Slice the leaves into 2- by ½-inch pieces.

When the onion is tender and the pancetta is crisp, add the red wine to the pan and deglaze, stirring to scrape up any bits that may have stuck to the bottom. Add the radicchio a little at a time, stirring until it is slightly wilted. Sprinkle with salt and a few tablespoons of water to moisten, then bring to a simmer. Cover and simmer until the radicchio is tender, 5 to 10 minutes.

Combine the cream, balsamic vinegar, and sugar in a small bowl. Add the mixture to the cooked radicchio with salt and pepper and simmer gently for about 30 seconds. Add the drained pasta to the pan and enough of the reserved pasta cooking water to achieve a saucy consistency and stir for a minute to combine.

Stir 2 tablespoons of the Parmesan cheese into the pasta, taste, and adjust the seasoning with salt and pepper. Place in shallow bowls and top each serving with pecans, a little more Parmesan, and a generous grinding of pepper.

---

40 minutes

Serves 6

- 1 pound penne rigate (see page 69)
- 2 tablespoons extra virgin olive oil
- ½ onion, diced
- 4 ounces sliced pancetta, diced
- 1 large head radicchio (about 12 ounces)
- ¼ cup dry red wine or water
- Salt and freshly ground black pepper to taste
- ⅓ cup heavy whipping cream
- 1 tablespoon balsamic vinegar, or to taste
- ½ teaspoon sugar, or to taste
- 3 tablespoons grated Parmesan cheese
- ¼ cup pecan halves, chopped

PER SERVING:
339 calories, 9 g protein, 28 g carbohydrate, 20 g fat (7 g saturated), 34 mg cholesterol, 434 mg sodium, 2 g fiber

Protein and Vegetarian Cooking

Many meat eaters assume that vegetarians don't get enough protein, but the truth is that, on average, Americans eat far more protein than they need. According to the U.S. National Academy of Sciences, healthy people need about 0.8 grams of protein per kilogram of body weight, which is just under 0.4 grams for every pound. A 150-pound woman, then, needs about 55 grams of protein per day, while a 170-pound man needs about 62 grams. The recipes in this chapter contain around 10 to 30 grams of protein per serving. If you also were to eat foods such as two slices of cheese (10 grams), four slices of bread (3 grams each), 2 eggs (12 to 16 grams), and 1 cup of yogurt (10 grams), you could easily reach your daily protein requirements.

The following lists the amount of protein in several foods that are often used as meat substitutes in this book:

Ingredient	Amount	Protein
Tofu	4 ounces	7.4 g
Chickpeas	½ cup cooked	7 g
Pine nuts	1 ounce	7 g
Eggs	1	6-8 g
Parmesan cheese	1 ounce	10 g

Vegetarian Meals

Many readers of my column, vegetarians and meat-eaters alike, ask for quick, meatless recipes. (See page 171 for an index of all the vegetarian recipes in the previous chapters.)

But "quick" and "vegetarian" can be a challenge, because washing, peeling, and cutting up vegetables can take a lot of time. Tofu can be prepared quickly, but beans, another vegetarian standby, can require hours to cook if they're prepared from scratch.

Washed and precut vegetables, from jicama sticks to chopped onions, that are available in grocery stores can help cut the preparation time. Unfortunately, some are treated with chemicals to preserve their freshness and might not have as much flavor or nutrition as freshly prepared foods. Also, they tend to cost a lot more than the same ingredients sold unwashed or uncut. But some of these products, such as prewashed and trimmed spinach, can really cut down on preparation time and are worth the extra cost.

Thai Red Curry with Sweet Potato, Tofu & Spinach (recipe on page 92)

35 minutes

Serves 4

1/3 cup pepitas or
sliced almonds
(see Note, page 47)

1 teaspoon vegetable oil

1/2 small red onion, diced

1 poblano chile,
seeded and diced

Kernels from 1 large
ear fresh corn, or
1/2 cup frozen,
prepared according to
package directions

Salt to taste

1 cup crumbled queso
fresco (about
4 ounces)
(see Note, page 26)

1 cup pre-grated
Monterey Jack cheese
(about 4 ounces)

Large pinch of dried
oregano, crumbled

8 taco-size flour tortillas

Fresh tomatillo salsa
for serving

Quesadillas with Poblanos, Corn & Pepitas

Full of crunchy pepitas (shelled green pumpkin seeds), fruity-spicy poblano peppers, and fresh cheese, these quesadillas are quite filling. Serve with a salad for dinner; if serving as an appetizer, cut them into wedges, though be careful, as the filling tends to fall out, since they aren't loaded with too much gooey cheese. (See photo on page 12.)

Preheat the oven to 250°F.

Toast the pepitas in a small, heavy frying pan over medium-low heat until they start popping, about 3 minutes. Shake a few times and continue cooking until most of the seeds are popped. Stir or toss frequently to avoid scorching. Remove from the heat and leave in the pan to finish cooking. If using almonds, toast in a pan over medium-low heat until golden, about 8 minutes, flipping once or twice.

Heat the oil in a frying pan over medium heat. Add the onion and cook until just softened, about 3 minutes. Add the chile and corn. Sauté, stirring occasionally, until tender, about 5 minutes. Season with salt and remove from the heat.

Combine the queso fresco and Monterey Jack in a small bowl with the oregano and the cooled toasted pepitas.

Heat a large griddle or two clean frying pans over medium-low heat. Gently fold four of the tortillas and place on the griddle, or place two in each pan, so that only half of each tortilla is touching the pan. Stuff each tortilla with 1/4 cup of the vegetable mixture and 1/4 cup of the cheese mixture.

Cook until browned, about 3 minutes, then carefully flip the tortillas, folded side down, and continue cooking until the cheese is gooey and the bottom of the tortilla is browned, about 2 minutes. Place the finished quesadillas on a baking sheet in the oven and repeat with the remaining ingredients. Serve hot, passing the tomatillo salsa at the table.

> **NOTE:** Poblano chiles are available in Latin American markets and in many supermarkets. Mildly spicy, the chiles are blackish-green and rounded at the stem but narrow and pointy at the tip. Seed and dice as you would a bell pepper.

PER SERVING: 471 calories,
23 g protein, 45 g carbohydrate,
24 g fat (9 g saturated),
34 mg cholesterol,
477 mg sodium, 2 g fiber

Mushroom Marsala with Polenta

This recipe uses precooked polenta, which you can find in a refrigerated case in most supermarkets. The creamy, vegetarian ragout is enlivened with marsala wine and contrasts well with the crisp rounds of polenta. If you like, serve it with Stir-Fried Greens (see page 162).

Heat the oven to 450°F. Position an oven rack 4-6 inches from the heating element. Lightly grease a small baking sheet with some butter.

Melt the 2 tablespoons butter in a large sauté pan over medium heat. Add the garlic and thyme and sauté until fragrant, about 1 minute. Add all the mushrooms and season with salt and pepper. Sauté, stirring often, until tender, 6 to 8 minutes.

Meanwhile, slice the polenta into eight ½-inch-thick rounds (you will have one-third of the roll left over; save it for another use). Arrange the polenta rounds on the prepared baking sheet and place on the oven rack. Bake 5 minutes, then sprinkle about ½ tablespoon Parmesan on top of each slice and return to the oven until brown and crisp, 2 to 3 minutes more.

When the mushrooms are tender, increase the heat to high and stir in the marsala. When the mixture is almost dry, add the broth. Bring to a simmer, then reduce the heat to medium-low and stir in the cream. Heat through, taste, and adjust the amount of salt and pepper, if necessary.

To serve, transfer the polenta slices to shallow bowls. Ladle the ragout over the polenta and top with the remaining Parmesan and the chives.

30 minutes

Serves 4

- 2 tablespoons unsalted butter
- 2 cloves garlic, minced
- ½ teaspoon dried thyme
- 1 pound button or crimini mushrooms, diced
- 8 ounces shiitake mushrooms, stemmed and diced
- 3 portobello mushrooms, stemmed and diced

  Salt and freshly ground pepper to taste

- 1 35-ounce roll prepared polenta

  About ½ cup pre-grated Parmesan cheese

- ½ cup marsala wine
- ½ cup low-sodium vegetable broth
- ½ cup heavy whipping cream
- ½ bunch chives, cut into ½-inch lengths

PER SERVING: 372 calories, 11 g protein, 30 g carbohydrate, 21 g fat (12 g saturated), 64 mg cholesterol, 260 mg sodium, 7 g fiber

30 minutes

Serves 4

5   large portobello
    mushrooms (about
    1¼ pounds total),
    cleaned

3   tablespoons olive oil

2   cloves garlic, slivered

1   tablespoon
    balsamic vinegar

    Salt and freshly
    ground pepper
    to taste

1   large loaf unsliced
    crusty black olive
    bread or country-style
    French bread (about
    16 ounces)

2   ounces
    pecorino cheese

2   large jarred or fresh
    roasted bell peppers,
    cut into 4 large, flat
    pieces

4   ounces mixed
    baby greens

2   ounces alfalfa or
    daikon sprouts
    (optional; see Note,
    page 56)

PER SERVING: 508 calories,
21 g protein, 67 g carbohydrate,
17 g fat (4 g saturated),
10 mg cholesterol,
1,041 mg sodium, 9 g fiber

Portobello Burgers with Shaved Pecorino

Vegetarians often lose out at summer barbecues. Although garden burgers can be delicious, they can also char and stick to the grill, and tofu dogs don't do much for me unless they're smothered in ketchup. Grilled portobello mushrooms are my favorite vegetarian barbecue alternative. In this recipe, the meaty mushrooms are layered with roasted bell peppers, pecorino cheese, and crisp salad greens between slices of toasty olive bread.

If you plan to use a grill, prepare a fire or preheat a gas grill for cooking over medium heat. Or preheat the oven to 500°F and line a baking sheet with aluminum foil.

Cut off the stems from the portobellos and brush the top of the caps lightly with some of the olive oil. Place the portobellos stem side up on a work surface. Slip the garlic slivers into the mushroom gills.

Whisk together the remaining olive oil and the balsamic vinegar. Drizzle or brush a few teaspoons of this vinaigrette on the mushroom gills and season with salt and pepper.

If you are using a grill, place the mushrooms stem side up directly on the grill. If you are using the oven, place the mushrooms stem side up on the prepared baking sheet. Cook the mushrooms until they are tender and juicy, 10 to 15 minutes. Keep warm by wrapping with foil.

While the mushrooms are cooking, slice the bread into 8 slices 1 inch thick each. Toast on the grill or in the oven for about 5 minutes, turning once.

Trim the rind off the pecorino cheese. Hold a piece of cheese firmly against a cutting board with a narrow end up. Using a sturdy vegetable peeler, and without pressing too hard, shave off very thin slices of the cheese. Shave enough slices for two layers in each sandwich and set aside.

To assemble the sandwiches, drizzle each piece of toast lightly with the remaining vinaigrette. Place a folded piece of red pepper on the bottom of each sandwich, then top with a layer of pecorino. Add enough hot portobellos to cover (you may have to cut the mushrooms to fit). Place more shaved pecorino on top of each mushroom, then top with some baby greens and sprouts. Top with the remaining bread and serve at once.

NOTE: You can find prepared roasted bell peppers near the jarred olives in many supermarkets. Using bell pepper strips is also fine.

TIP: Pecorino is often shaved onto foods because the cheese's briny flavor and delicate, granular texture are best appreciated when it's served in thin slivers.

Roasted Portobello Mushrooms with Panzanella

Panzanella is a Tuscan salad of dry bread, tomatoes, and herbs. This version uses focaccia because it's already crisp, so it toasts up quickly, and it has lots of flavor from the olive oil and coarse salt it contains. The mushrooms piled high with colorful panzanella make a graceful entree for a vegetarian dinner party. You could also buy six smaller portobellos and present them as a first course for six; there's enough panzanella to go around.

Preheat the oven to 450°F. Position one oven rack at the top of the oven, near the heating element, and a second rack at least 5 inches below it.

Place the mushrooms stem side up on a baking sheet, sprinkle with salt and pepper, and roast on the top rack of the oven until very soft, 20 to 25 minutes.

Meanwhile, spread the bread cubes in a baking pan and place on the bottom rack of the oven. Toast for 5 minutes, then shake the pan to stir the cubes. Continue toasting until crisp, 3 minutes more. Let cool briefly.

Combine the tomatoes, onion, Gorgonzola, chopped basil, and capers in a large salad bowl. When the bread is ready, add it to the top.

Place the vinegar in a small bowl, season with salt and pepper, and whisk in the olive oil. Pour this dressing over the bread salad, tossing as you pour. Season with salt and pepper and toss again gently. Let sit for a few minutes before serving.

Place the greens on serving plates, top each serving with a mushroom, and then pile the bread salad on top. Garnish with basil leaves and serve.

[**NOTE:** Plain focaccia is often available in the bakery or deli sections of supermarkets. One containing a little onion or garlic is fine, but don't get focaccia with pizza toppings.]

---

35 minutes

Serves 4

- 4 large portobello mushrooms (1 pound total), cleaned and stems removed

  Salt and freshly ground pepper to taste

- 8 ounces plain focaccia, cut into large cubes (about 4 cups)

- 2 firm but ripe tomatoes, diced

- ½ medium red onion, cut into small dice

- 3 ounces crumbled Gorgonzola cheese

- 2 tablespoons finely chopped fresh basil, plus basil leaves for garnish

- 1 tablespoon drained capers

- 2 tablespoons red wine vinegar

- 2 tablespoons extra virgin olive oil

  A few cups mixed salad greens

PER SERVING: 344 calories, 14 g protein, 40 g carbohydrate, 15 g fat (5 g saturated), 23 mg cholesterol, 673 mg sodium, 6 g fiber

Serves 4 to 6

1 cup cracked bulgur
wheat

½ teaspoon salt,
plus more to taste

1 large bunch fresh
Italian (flat-leaf)
parsley

5 green onions,
cut into thirds

Handful of fresh
mint leaves
(optional)

2 tablespoons fresh
lemon juice (from
about 1 lemon), plus
more to taste

¼ cup extra virgin
olive oil

Freshly ground
pepper to taste

1 small cucumber,
diced

½ pint cherry
tomatoes, halved

4 to 6 large pieces pita
bread, halved and
warmed

½ to ¾ cup prepared
hummus

PER SERVING: 326 calories,
9 g protein, 47 g carbohydrate,
12 g fat (1 g saturated),
0 g cholesterol, 498 mg sodium,
7 g fiber

Tabbouleh Salad with Pita & Hummus

*Preparing the salad takes less than 30 minutes, but it needs to chill before serving.
You can "flash-chill" it if you like (see Tip, page 32). There are plenty of instant boxed
versions of tabbouleh, a Middle Eastern dish of marinated bulgur wheat, herbs, and
vegetables, but because one of the main ingredients is parsley, it's much more
delicious made fresh. Tabbouleh is refreshing and hearty at the same time, and when
you serve it with pita bread and store-bought hummus it makes a light meal. If you
like, substitute the hummus with Microwave Baba Ghanoush (see page 164).*

Place the bulgur, ½ teaspoon salt, and 1½ cups water in a saucepan and
bring to a boil. Reduce the heat to a simmer, cover, and cook until al dente,
about 13 minutes, or follow the package directions. Immediately spread the
cooked bulgur onto a baking sheet to cool.

Meanwhile, cut off the main parsley stems, then cut the remainder of the
bunch, both leaves and tender stems, into thirds. Combine the parsley with the
green onions and the mint, if using, in a food processor and pulse until finely
chopped.

In a large salad bowl, whisk together the 2 tablespoons lemon juice, olive oil,
and salt and pepper to taste. Add the bulgur, parsley mixture, cucumber, and
tomatoes and stir to combine. If needed, add salt, pepper, and more lemon
juice to taste. Chill for a few hours or overnight or "flash chill."

To serve, let diners help themselves, scooping tabbouleh into pita pockets
and topping with hummus.

NOTE: Cracked bulgur wheat can be found in specialty supermarkets
or health food stores, either in bulk or boxed; I like the whole-wheat
version.

30 minutes

Serves 4

2 cups falafel mix

½ cup low-fat plain yogurt

¼ cup tahini

Juice of 1 lemon, or to taste

1 small clove garlic, finely minced

¼ teaspoon salt, plus more to taste

¼ teaspoon cayenne pepper

1 ripe tomato, diced

Leaves from 6 sprigs fresh Italian (flat-leaf) parsley (optional)

4 ounces baby greens

Canola oil for frying

4 to 6 large pieces pita bread, halved and warmed

Falafel Sandwiches with Tahini Yogurt Sauce

Even though it helped me get through college, I'd almost forgotten about instant falafel mix until recently. The crunchy, savory balls just need a few fixings, like tomatoes, greens, and an easy tahini sauce, to be elevated to the status of a home-cooked meal. This recipe is meant to be served family style, which means diners put together their own falafel sandwiches. For a Middle Eastern feast with friends, serve with Tabbouleh Salad with Pita & Hummus (page 88).

Put the falafel mix in a bowl and stir in the amount of water indicated in the package directions. Set aside for 15 minutes.

Meanwhile, combine the yogurt, tahini, half the lemon juice, the garlic, the ¼ teaspoon salt, and cayenne pepper in a bowl. If necessary, add a few teaspoons of water to achieve a sauce-like consistency. Transfer the sauce to a serving bowl.

Toss together the tomato, parsley, if using, greens, and remaining lemon juice in a serving bowl. Set aside.

Pour the canola oil in a sauté pan to a depth of about ½ inch. Heat over medium heat while you form the falafel balls. Set out a platter lined with paper towels.

Roll the falafel mixture into balls about 2 inches in diameter. Flatten the balls so they're about 1 inch thick. You should have about 16 balls total.

When the oil is hot, working in batches as necessary to avoid crowding, add the falafel balls and fry, turning once, until golden brown and puffy on both sides, 6 to 8 minutes total. Using a slotted spoon, transfer to the paper towels to drain. Repeat with the remaining falafel balls.

To serve, bring everything to the table and let diners help themselves, filling their pitas with falafels and vegetables, then topping with the tahini sauce.

[**NOTE:** Tahini, a paste made of ground sesame seeds, is available at Middle Eastern, health food, and gourmet grocery stores.]

PER SERVING: 625 calories, 29 g protein, 97 g carbohydrate, 16 g fat (2 g saturated), 2 mg cholesterol, 658 mg sodium, 21 g fiber

TIP: Falafel mix is available in health food stores and supermarkets. Don't use too high a heat to fry the falafels or they will brown on the outside while remaining raw on the inside. It's a good idea to cut one in half to test it before you remove all of them from the pan. You can always make a few extra falafels because they stay crisp even when reheated the next day.

Fried Rice with Tofu, Shiitake & Bok Choy

Unlike many recipes for fried rice, this one is more of a main course than a side dish because it contains more vegetables and tofu than rice itself. Make this dish when you have leftover home-cooked or takeout rice you'd like to use up. If you don't have any, cook 1 cup of medium-grain rice, spread it out on a baking sheet to cool, and refrigerate it as long as possible before frying it. If the rice is hot and freshly cooked, it will become mushy when you stir-fry it.

Beat the eggs with the sesame oil, salt, and pepper in a small bowl. Set aside.

Heat 1 tablespoon of the vegetable oil in a wok or large nonstick frying pan over medium-high heat. Add the chiles; stir for a few moments, then add the bok choy. Stir-fry until just wilted, 1 to 2 minutes.

Increase the heat to high, then add the mushrooms and green onions. Season with salt and stir-fry until the dense part of the bok choy is tender and the mushroom pieces are moist and reduced in size, 2 to 4 minutes. Remove the vegetables from the wok.

Reduce the heat to medium-high and add the remaining 1 tablespoon of the vegetable oil to the wok. When it is hot, add the rice, breaking it up in the pan. Stir-fry until the grains are separate.

Push the rice to the edges of the wok. Add the egg mixture to the center of the wok. Let it set for a minute or so, then turn it and let the other side set. Continue stir-frying until the eggs are dry and mixed into the rice.

Add the tofu and soy sauce mixture to the wok and stir-fry until the tofu is warm and most of the liquid has evaporated. Stir in the vegetables. Serve at once, garnished with a few chiles, if using.

> **NOTE:** Delicately flavored and crunchy, bok choy is one of the Chinese cabbages available in Asian markets and many supermarkets. Soak the bok choy in a large bowl of water to remove all the sand before slicing it. You can find marinated and baked tofu in refrigerated sections of many supermarkets.

30 minutes

Serves 4

- 2 large eggs
- 1 teaspoon Asian sesame oil

  Salt and freshly ground pepper to taste
- 2 tablespoons vegetable oil
- 2 small dried red chiles or ½ teaspoon red pepper flakes
- 8 ounces baby bok choy or napa cabbage, trimmed and sliced into ribbons about ½ inch thick
- 8 ounces shiitake mushrooms, stemmed and cut into large dice
- 3 green onions, thinly sliced
- 3 cups cold, leftover steamed white rice
- 4 ounces marinated and baked tofu, cubed
- 2 tablespoons soy sauce mixed with 1 tablespoon water

  Small dried red chiles for garnish (optional)

PER SERVING: 340 calories, 14 g protein, 39 carbohydrate, 15 g fat (2 g saturated), 106 mg cholesterol, 657 mg sodium, 5 g fiber

35 minutes

Serves 4

1 tablespoon
vegetable oil

1 onion, diced

1 cup low-sodium
vegetable broth

1 13.5-ounce can
"lite" coconut milk

2 tablespoons
Asian fish sauce

1 tablespoon
Thai red curry paste

1 sweet potato,
peeled and diced

14 ounces firm tofu,
cut into 1-inch cubes

4 to 5 ounces pre-washed
spinach

Thai Red Curry with Sweet Potato, Tofu & Spinach

Thai food is known for its fiery heat, but what makes it so delicious is the interplay of hot chiles, salty fish sauce, sour citrus, and sweet ingredients. Although coconut milk often sweetens Thai dishes, vegetables also play a role. The sweet potato in this dish tames the heat of the curry paste. Serve with steamed jasmine rice. (See photo on page 83.)

Heat the oil in a sauté pan over medium heat. Add the onion and sauté, stirring occasionally, until tender, about 8 minutes. Add the broth, coconut milk, and fish sauce. Bring to a simmer, add the curry paste, and stir until dissolved.

Add the sweet potato and simmer until almost tender, about 10 minutes. Add the tofu and simmer until heated through, 3 to 4 minutes. Stir in the spinach a handful at a time, cooking until it wilts. Serve at once.

[**NOTE:** Thai red curry paste is available in Asian markets and in many supermarkets. Its heat level varies, so start by using a small quantity and add more to taste.]

PER SERVING: 295 calories,
19 g protein, 22 g carbohydrate,
17 g fat (5 g saturated),
0 mg cholesterol, 429 mg sodium,
5 g fiber

Chickpea Curry with Watercress

This dish is so quick and easy to make that it may soon become a part of your weekly repertoire. The curry-enhanced coconut milk sauce gives the canned chickpeas a lift, and the watercress adds a peppery note. Serve with basmati rice and, if you like, warm naan, an Indian bread.

Melt the butter in a large sauté pan over medium-low heat. Add the curry powder and red pepper flakes and cook, stirring constantly, until lightly toasted, about 5 minutes. Add the onion, increase heat to medium, and cook until translucent but still a little crunchy, about 5 minutes. Add the chickpeas, tomatoes, and coconut milk. Stir and simmer until the flavors are melded, about 3 minutes. Add ½ cup water if necessary to thin the sauce.

While the curry simmers, trim off the thick stems of the watercress. Coarsely chop the rest of the watercress. Add to the curry, return to a simmer, and cook until just wilted but still bright green, about 1 minute. Serve at once.

NOTE: Watercress resembles arugula, with thicker stems, and is found at many supermarkets with the other fresh herbs and lettuces. Tender and mild upland cress (usually sold with the roots still attached) is too delicate for this dish. If you can't find regular watercress, substitute several cups of arugula leaves.

25 minutes

Serves 4

- 1 tablespoon unsalted butter
- 2 tablespoons curry powder
- ¼ teaspoon red pepper flakes
- 1 onion, diced
- 2 15-ounce cans chickpeas, drained and rinsed, or 3 cups freshly cooked chickpeas
- 1 14½-ounce can chopped no-added-salt tomatoes, drained
- 1 cup canned "lite" coconut milk, can shaken before measuring
- ½ bunch watercress

PER SERVING: 306 calories, 11 g protein, 43 g carbohydrate, 12 g fat (5 g saturated), 8 mg cholesterol, 461 mg sodium, 13 g fiber

TOFU

14	ounces firm tofu
1/3	cup rice wine or dry sherry
3	tablespoons soy sauce
1 1/2	tablespoons unseasoned rice vinegar or cider vinegar
2	teaspoons Asian sesame oil
2	tablespoons minced fresh ginger
1	teaspoon sugar
	Vegetable oil for brushing

PEANUT NOODLES

12	ounces fresh Asian-style noodles, preferably thin (see Note, page 39)
1/4	cup natural chunky peanut butter
1/2	teaspoon chile paste, or to taste
1/2	teaspoon sugar, or to taste
2 to 3	green onions (including most of the green parts), thinly sliced
1	red jalapeño chile, seeded and very thinly sliced (optional)
1/4	cup reserved tofu marinade

PER SERVING: 465 calories, 21 g protein, 73 g carbohydrate, 13 g fat (2 g saturated), 0 mg cholesterol, 541 mg sodium, 13 g fiber

Grilled Tofu with Cool Peanut Noodles

The chile paste and jalapeño in this recipe make the noodles fairly spicy, but they help balance the sweetness and richness of the peanut sauce. Serve with steamed bok choy or broccoli drizzled with the reserved marinade.

If you plan to use a grill, prepare a fire or preheat a gas grill for cooking over medium heat. (You can also use an oiled grill pan over medium-high heat.) Bring a large pot of water to a boil for the noodles.

To prepare the tofu, drain it and pat it dry. Slice 1/2 inch thick. Combine the wine, soy sauce, 3 tablespoons water, vinegar, sesame oil, ginger, and sugar in a large, shallow casserole dish. Add the tofu, making sure it's submerged, and marinate for 20 to 30 minutes.

Remove the tofu from the marinade, reserving 1/4 cup of the marinade. Brush the grill with some vegetable oil, then place the tofu diagonally across the grill grate. Grill until browned on the bottom, 3 to 5 minutes, then turn and grill until browned on the second side, 3 to 5 minutes more. Watch carefully because tofu burns easily.

To prepare the peanut noodles, cook the noodles according to the package directions, then rinse in cool water and drain.

Combine the peanut butter, 1/4 cup water, chile paste, sugar, green onions, and jalapeño in a bowl. Stir in the reserved tofu marinade. The sauce will seem thin. Toss with the noodles, adding a little water if necessary to coat the noodles evenly.

To serve, arrange 2 or 3 pieces of tofu over each serving of noodles.

TIP: To save time when making this recipe, buy a jar of Thai or other Asian peanut sauce and use 1/2 cup plus a few tablespoons instead of making the peanut sauce.

Chinese Noodles
with Five-Spice Shiitake Mushrooms

30 minutes

Serves 4

Five-spice powder is a Chinese spice mixture made of ground star anise, cinnamon, fennel seeds, cloves, and ginger or Sichuan peppercorns. Heady and rich, it brings an intense earthiness to many Chinese dishes, especially braised ones, and complements shiitake mushrooms extremely well. Soaking dried shiitakes creates an instant broth that intensifies the stir-fry sauce for the noodles.

Bring a large pot of water to a boil for the noodles. When it is boiling, cook the noodles until tender according to the package directions. Drain the noodles, rinse under cold running water, and drain well again.

Meanwhile, bring 2½ cups water to a boil in a small sauce pan. Add the dried shiitakes, cover, and simmer for 3 minutes. Strain the liquid through a paper coffee filter into bowl to remove any grit, then squeeze the mushrooms over the bowl. Roughly chop the mushrooms, then set aside with the liquid.

Heat the butter and vegetable oil in a wok or large saucepan over medium heat. Add the five-spice powder and shallots and sauté, stirring frequently, until tender, about 2 minutes. Add the garlic and sauté 2 minutes more.

Increase the heat to medium-high and add both the fresh and reconstituted dry shiitakes with ½ cup of the reserved mushroom-soaking water. Cook, stirring frequently, until the mushrooms are tender, about 3 minutes. Add the soy sauce and rice wine. Increase the heat to high and cook, stirring, for 1 minute. Add the remaining mushroom-soaking water.

Add the noodles to the wok and stir until heated through and coated with the sauce, about 1 minute. Garnish with the green onions and sesame seeds and serve at once.

12	ounces fresh Asian-style noodles (see Note, page 39)
½	ounce dried shiitake mushrooms
1	tablespoon unsalted butter
1	tablespoon vegetable oil
1	teaspoon five-spice powder
2	shallots, minced
2	cloves garlic, minced
⅓	pound fresh shiitake mushrooms, stemmed and thinly sliced
2	tablespoons soy sauce
1	tablespoon Shaoxing rice wine or dry sherry
2	green onions, thinly sliced
1	tablespoon sesame seeds (optional)

TIP: To speed up the preparation, begin cooking the noodles and rehydrating the dried mushrooms before you chop the vegetables. Make sure you have all the stir-fry ingredients ready before you heat up your wok.

PER SERVING: 345 calories, 11 g protein, 56 g carbohydrate, 8 g fat (2 g saturated), 70 mg cholesterol, 477 mg sodium, 5 g fiber

Fish and Shellfish

A nice piece of fish is the basis for one of the best last-minute dinners. As long as it's impeccably fresh, most fish simply needs the right seasoning and a quick cooking method that won't dry it out.

Fattier fish like salmon and tuna are naturally rich and moist, so they don't need heavy, creamy sauces. It's better to pair them with slightly acidic sauces or a refreshing salad. They also do well on the grill or under the broiler since they don't dry out as quickly as leaner types of fish.

Mild-tasting lean white fish such as red snapper, catfish, and sole are often paired with classic butter- or mayonnaise-based sauces. The delicate texture of their thin fillets means that they are usually best quickly sautéed or pan-fried.

Some fish are more versatile. Pacific cod, sea bass, and halibut, for example, are excellent braised and steamed, their snowy white flesh becoming succulent in the moist heat, yet they also do well under the broiler or in the frying pan.

No matter which of the following dishes you choose to make, be flexible at the seafood market and pick out whatever is freshest rather than precisely what is listed in the recipe. Shop at stores with a high turnover and knowledgeable staff, and plan to cook fish the day you buy it or, at the very latest, the next. Choose fillets that are shiny and firm, with no dryness around the edges. The fish shouldn't smell overly fishy but pleasantly of the sea.

Unfortunately, many popular fish and shellfish are being fished or farmed in ways that are extremely harmful to the environment, not to mention your health. In the following pages I provide some tips about how to avoid problematic seafood, but environmental recommendations change frequently. Seek out resources that can help you make informed choices about the fish and shellfish you eat, such as the Seafood Watch Web site from the Monterey Bay Aquarium, *www.mbayaq.org/cr/seafoodwatch.asp*.

Facing page: Broiled Swordfish with Saffron Orzo & Charmoula (recipe on page 108); Wasabi Pea-Crusted Fish (recipe on page 116)

25 minutes

Serves 4

2 small heads
  Belgian endive

4 small radishes,
  thinly sliced

1 cup cherry tomatoes,
  halved

1 green onion,
  sliced diagonally

2 sprigs fresh thyme,
  finely chopped
  (2 to 4 teaspoons
  chopped)

4 wild salmon fillets,
  6 to 7 ounces each
  and 1 inch thick,
  pinbones removed

  Salt and freshly
  ground pepper
  to taste

1 to 2 tablespoons
  vegetable oil

1 firm but ripe avocado,
  cubed (see Tip,
  page 32)

1 tablespoon fresh
  lemon juice

Seared Salmon
with Avocado-Endive Salad

In this recipe you sear the salmon until it develops a beautiful golden crust, then serve it with a creamy yet refreshing avocado-endive salad. Endive and radish add some bitter and spicy notes to the rich avocado and fish, and thyme makes everything taste fresh. For more tips on searing, see page 15.

Trim the end off the endive, separate the leaves, and chop into 1-inch pieces. Toss the endive, radishes, tomatoes, green onion, and 1 teaspoon of the thyme together in a salad bowl.

Season the salmon with salt and pepper to taste. Coat the top of each fillet with the remaining thyme.

Heat a large frying pan over medium-high heat. When the pan is hot, add the oil and heat until it shimmers. Add 2 salmon fillets to the pan, flesh side down, and cook until crispy on the bottom, 2 to 2½ minutes. Turn the fillets and cook 2 to 2½ minutes more. The fish should be slightly rare in the center and crispy outside. Increase the cooking time to about 3 minutes per side if you prefer your fish cooked to medium. Remove the fillets from the pan and let rest, tented with foil, for a few minutes. Repeat with remaining fillets.

While the fish is cooking, add the avocado cubes to the salad along with the lemon juice, salt, and pepper. Fold the avocado into the salad very gently to prevent it from getting mushy. Taste and adjust the amount of salt and pepper. Distribute the salmon and the salad among serving plates and serve at once.

> **NOTE:** Belgian endive is a small yellow chicory sold near salad greens in most markets. When shopping for it, look for bunches that are light yellow and without a lot of brown spots. Endive should be stored protected from light, which can cause discoloration.

PER SERVING: 295 calories, 30 g protein, 7 g carbohydrate, 16 g fat (3 g saturated), 66 mg cholesterol, 86 mg sodium, 4 g fiber

TIP: Tweezers or needle-nose pliers are effective tools in removing pinbones from fish.

Salmon with Leeks & Bok Choy

This dish celebrates springtime with a colorful display of Easter-egg colors like pink-orange fish and spring-green leeks. Seasoning the vegetables with rice vinegar and lemon zest gives them a pickled flavor that suits the richness of roasted salmon. Though the bok choy should be wilted, take care not to overcook it or it will lose its delicate, juicy crunch. Serve this dish with steamed medium-grain rice.

Preheat the broiler and place the rack about 4 inches from the heating element. Line a baking sheet with aluminum foil.

Melt the butter in a large sauté pan over medium heat. Add the red pepper flakes and stir for a few seconds. Add the leeks and sauté, stirring occasionally, until soft, 10 minutes.

While the leeks are cooking, season the salmon fillets with salt and pepper. Place on the prepared baking sheet and broil until the salmon flakes but is still slightly pink in the middle, about 7 minutes. Remove from the heat, tent with foil, and let rest 5 minutes.

When the leeks are soft, add the bok choy, vinegar, and lemon zest. Season with salt. Cover and wilt for 2 minutes, stirring once. Taste and adjust the amount of salt.

Arrange the vegetables and their juice in shallow soup bowls and top with the salmon. Sprinkle with the sesame seeds, if using, and serve.

20 minutes

Serves 4

- 2 tablespoons unsalted butter
- Pinch of red pepper flakes
- 1 leek, cleaned and thinly sliced (about 8 ounces)
- 4 wild salmon fillets, 6 to 7 ounces each and 1 inch thick, pinbones removed
- Salt and freshly ground pepper to taste
- 1 pound baby bok choy, stemmed and sliced crosswise into 1/4-inch strips (see Note, page 91)
- 2 tablespoons unseasoned rice vinegar
- 1/2 teaspoon grated lemon zest
- 1 teaspoon black sesame seeds (optional)

TIP: To clean and slice leeks, leaving the stem attached, slice the leek in half lengthwise and clean thoroughly under running water, using your fingers to spread the leaves to remove the grit hidden between them. Remove the stem and slice the leek across the grain into very thin strips until you reach the dark green part. Peel away layers of the leek to reveal lighter green parts underneath, and continue until you've finished cutting all the light green parts.

PER SERVING: 268 calories, 36 g protein, 3 g carbohydrate, 12 g fat (5 g saturated), 95 mg cholesterol, 159 mg sodium, 2 g fiber

30 minutes

Serves 4

1 tablespoon unsalted butter or olive oil

1 spring onion or 3 green onions, sliced

1¼ cups quinoa, rinsed and drained if necessary

½ teaspoon salt, plus more to taste

8 ounces English peas in the pod, or about ½ cup frozen peas

4 wild salmon fillets, 6 to 7 ounces each and 1 inch thick, pinbones removed

Freshly ground pepper to taste

Lemon wedges for serving

PER SERVING: 525 calories, 42 g protein, 45 g carbohydrate, 19 g fat (5 g saturated), 110 mg cholesterol, 388 mg sodium, 6 g fiber

Broiled Salmon with Quinoa & Peas

Both peas and wild salmon are in season in early spring, so they make good partners. Adding a nutty quinoa pilaf packs this simple and delicious dish with nutrients. Spring onions, if available, are a nice touch.

Preheat the broiler, placing the rack about 4 inches from the heating element. Line a baking sheet with aluminum foil.

Melt the butter in a sauté pan over medium heat, then sauté the onions until tender, about 3 minutes. Add the quinoa, 2½ cups water, and ½ teaspoon salt. Bring to a simmer, cover, and cook until the water is absorbed, 10 to 15 minutes. Remove from the heat and let rest a few minutes.

While the quinoa is cooking, shell the peas if using English peas. Add the fresh or frozen peas to the pan about 5 minutes before the quinoa is done.

Season the salmon fillets with salt and pepper. Place on the prepared baking sheet and broil until the salmon flakes but is still slightly pink in the middle, about 7 minutes. Remove from the heat, tent with foil, and let rest 5 minutes.

Arrange the fish on top of the quinoa on serving plates and serve with lemon wedges.

NOTE: Quinoa (see box) is available in health food stores and in some grocery stores. Some brands needs to be rinsed while others don't; follow the package directions.

WHOLE GRAINS AND QUINOA

Nutrition experts tout the benefit of whole grains, encouraging us to eat more of them in place of "empty" starches such as white bread, white rice, and pasta to control weight and reduce the risk of disease. Whole grains contain more fiber and protein than other grains.

But it can be intimidating to tackle those earnest-looking brown kernels such as kasha, barley, bulgur wheat, and millet, found in natural-food stores and some supermarkets. Some of these grains, such as brown rice, take longer to cook than more refined grains, which can discourage cooks with limited time.

Quinoa (pronounced KEEN-wah) is quick-cooking and versatile. Though it's a seed, quinoa acts like a grain in many dishes. It cooks in 10 to 15 minutes, has an intriguing nutty flavor, and, because it has eight essential amino acids, is considered a complete protein. It also offers a high dose of iron, potassium, and B vitamins.

Quinoa was prized by the Incas and Aztecs and remains a staple in South America. To prepare it, rinse it in a fine-mesh strainer, if necessary, then cook it in twice its volume of water until it absorbs most of the liquid but is still slightly al dente. The moisture will continue to be absorbed as it rests.

1/2 cup nonfat
plain yogurt

2 tablespoons finely
chopped fresh
cilantro

1 teaspoon fresh
lemon juice

Salt and freshly
ground pepper
to taste

4 wild salmon fillets,
6 to 7 ounces each
and 1 inch thick,
pinbones removed

1 pound green beans,
trimmed

2 teaspoons
vegetable oil

1 teaspoon yellow
or brown mustard
seeds

1/2 teaspoon
ground cumin

1/8 to 1/4 teaspoon
cayenne pepper

Salmon with Spiced Green Beans & Yogurt Sauce

The toasted mustard seeds and smoky cumin on the beans and the creamy yogurt-cilantro sauce reveal an Indian influence on this recipe. When you heat whole mustard seeds, they pop, releasing their flavor and color into the cooking oil. The green beans will be on the spicy side if you use 1/4 teaspoon cayenne, but the yogurt sauce cools them down and is a nice accompaniment to the rich salmon. Serve with basmati rice.

Preheat the broiler, placing the rack about 4 inches from the heating element. Line a baking sheet with aluminum foil.

Combine the yogurt, cilantro, and lemon juice in a small bowl and season with salt and pepper.

Season the salmon with salt and pepper. Place on the prepared baking sheet and broil until the salmon flakes but is still slightly pink in the middle, about 7 minutes. Remove from the heat, tent with foil, and let rest 5 minutes.

Meanwhile, place the beans in a steamer and cook until crisp-tender, 5 to 8 minutes.

While the beans are cooking, heat the oil in a frying pan over medium-low heat. Add the mustard seeds, cumin, and cayenne. Sauté until the mustard seeds just start to pop, about 5 minutes. Add the green beans and cook, stirring, until heated through, 1 to 2 minutes. Season with salt.

To serve, divide the salmon and beans among individual plates and pass the sauce at the table.

PER SERVING: 376 calories, 38 g protein, 10 g carbohydrate, 20 g fat (4 g saturated), 112 mg cholesterol, 108 mg sodium, 2 g fiber

TIP: If you like, you can prepare the sauce and steam the green beans, shocking them in ice water when they become crisp-tender, up to a day in advance. From this point it will take only 10 to 15 minutes to broil the salmon and sauté the green beans.

Curried Prawns with Mangoes

This fresh-tasting California-influenced Chinese dish has a balance of spicy and sweet flavors. It's important to sauté dried spices such as curry powder in fat before adding other ingredients to avoid ending up with a raw, grainy flavor. Diners who don't like spicy food can opt to remove the large pieces of jalapeño. Serve with steamed rice and steamed or stir-fried vegetables.

Heat the oil in a large frying pan or wok over low heat. Add the curry powder and sauté, stirring occasionally, for 5 minutes. Add the onion and garlic to the pan, increase the heat to medium, and sauté until the onion is starting to become tender and translucent, about 5 minutes.

While the onion is cooking, toss the shrimp with ¼ teaspoon salt and a few pinches of pepper. Set aside.

When the onion has started to become tender, increase the heat to high, add the chile, and stir-fry until seared, 1 to 2 minutes. Add the shrimp and stir-fry until almost cooked through, 1 to 2 minutes. Add the mango and stir-fry another minute. Stir in the cilantro, then add a squeeze of lime juice. Season to taste with salt and serve at once.

> **NOTE:** Most shrimp you see in stores and on menus are farm-raised and imported from Asia. Unfortunately, these farms create widespread pollution and destruction of coastal mangroves. In general, trap-caught shrimp are best, but farmed or trawl-caught shrimp from the United States also are acceptable, because this country has more stringent fishing regulations.

20 minutes

Serves 4

- 4 teaspoons vegetable oil
- 2½ teaspoons curry powder
- 1 cup diced onion
- 1 small clove garlic, minced
- 1 pound peeled and deveined medium shrimp (see Note)
- ¼ teaspoon salt, plus more to taste
- Freshly ground pepper to taste
- 1 jalapeño chile, thickly sliced
- 1 large medium-ripe mango, cut into large dice
- 2 tablespoons coarsely chopped fresh cilantro
- ½ lime

TIP: An easy way to chop mango is to hold the fruit upright on a cutting board with a narrow side facing you. Using a large knife, cut down through fruit about ½ inch from the center, just grazing the side of the pit. Repeat on the other side. Score the exposed flesh in each half in a crisscross pattern, cutting down to the skin but not piercing it. Push against the center of the peel to turn the piece inside out, then use your chef's knife to cut off the mango cubes.

PER SERVING: 215 calories, 24 g protein, 14 g carbohydrate, 7 g fat (1 g saturated), 172 mg cholesterol, 437 mg sodium, 3 g fiber

30 minutes

Serves 4

6 cups chopped coleslaw mix or thinly shredded cabbage (about 8 ounces)

3/4 teaspoon freshly ground pepper

3 1/2 tablespoons fresh lime juice (from about 2 limes)

Salt to taste

1/2 cup plus 2 teaspoons vegetable oil

8 to 12 small corn tortillas

3 cloves garlic, minced

1 1/2 pounds peeled and deveined medium shrimp (see Note, page 103)

Mexican hot sauce or Tabasco sauce for serving

Mild tomato or fruit salsa for serving

Sour cream for serving

Shrimp Tacos with Black Pepper Slaw

This recipe is a version of the fish tacos popular in Baja California, with golden fried tortillas used to wrap up cool green cabbage slaw, rosy shrimp, spicy salsa, and sour cream. The slaw, with its rush of lime juice and freshly ground pepper, is an appealing counterpoint to the sweet, garlicky shrimp. The best part is when you bring all the colorful components to the table and invite diners to assemble their own tacos.

Preheat the oven to 250°F.

Toss the cabbage with the pepper and 3 tablespoons of the lime juice in a bowl, then season with salt. The slaw should be both tart and peppery. Set aside.

Line a baking sheet with paper towels. Heat 1/2 cup of the oil in a large frying pan over medium heat, until shimmering. Working in batches, quickly fry the tortillas until slightly crisp, about 30 seconds per side. Gently fold each tortilla in half and drain on the baking sheet, then keep warm in the oven.

Heat the remaining 2 teaspoons oil in a medium frying pan over medium-high heat. Add the garlic and sauté for 1 minute. Add the shrimp and sprinkle them with a few dashes of hot sauce and the remaining 1/2 tablespoon lime juice. Cook, stirring frequently, until the shrimp just begin to curl and turn pink, 2 to 3 minutes.

To serve, place the tortillas, shrimp, slaw, salsa, and sour cream in serving bowls and let diners assemble their own tacos.

PER SERVING: 560 calories, 44 g protein, 59 g carbohydrate, 19 g fat (2 g saturated), 259 mg cholesterol, 275 mg sodium, 11 g fiber

Fish in Spicy Saffron Broth with Couscous

This recipe is inspired by the flavors of a Moroccan tagine, a slow-cooked stew fragrant with spices. The fish and spices cook quickly yet make a surprisingly rich broth—perfect for the wheaty couscous to soak up. (See photo opposite title page.)

Chop the fish into 2-inch chunks. Combine the coriander, cumin, cayenne, paprika, and salt in a small bowl. Toss the fish with 1 tablespoon of the spice mixture and set aside to marinate at room temperature.

Bring a small pot of salted water to a boil for the couscous (use the amount specified in the package directions).

Heat the olive oil in a large sauté pan over medium heat. Add the onion and the remaining spice mixture and sauté until the onion is tender, about 8 minutes. Add the garlic and sauté for 1 minute more.

While the onion is sautéing, prepare the couscous according to the package directions and let rest as specified.

Add the broth and saffron mixture to the onions and bring to a simmer. Add the fish, cover, and keep at a simmer so the fish steams until flaky, 3 to 4 minutes. Taste and adjust the amount of salt.

Fluff the couscous with a fork, spoon it into shallow bowls, and ladle the stew over each serving, making sure to include plenty of the saffron broth in each bowl. Garnish with the cilantro or parsley and serve.

[**NOTE:** If you are going to use sea bass, look for a variety other than Chilean sea bass, which is severely overfished.]

30 minutes

Serves 4

1½ pounds skinless firm, mild white fish, such as halibut or Pacific sea bass

1 teaspoon ground coriander

1 teaspoon ground cumin

½ teaspoon cayenne pepper

1 teaspoon paprika

¾ teaspoon salt

3 tablespoons olive oil

1 onion, diced

4 cloves garlic, minced

1 cup instant couscous

1½ cups low-sodium fish or chicken broth

Pinch of saffron soaked in 2 tablespoons boiling water

2 tablespoons minced fresh cilantro or fresh Italian (flat-leaf) parsley

TIP: Don't let instant couscous sit too long after you've cooked it or it will begin to stick together.

PER SERVING: 468 calories, 42 g protein, 39 g carbohydrate, 15 g fat (3 g saturated), 54 mg cholesterol, 535 mg sodium, 3 g fiber

1 tablespoon Chinese
black beans, rinsed
and coarsely chopped

1 tablespoon soy sauce

1 teaspoon unseasoned
rice vinegar

1 teaspoon Chinese
rice wine or dry sherry

1 small clove garlic,
minced

1 teaspoon minced
fresh ginger

1 teaspoon vegetable oil

1 10- to 14-ounce fillet
of skinless Pacific
sea bass (see Note,
page 105), striped
bass, or halibut,
about 1 inch thick

Salt to taste

½ bunch medium-thick
asparagus, trimmed
and cut into 2-inch
lengths

Microwave-Steamed Sea Bass with Asparagus & Black Bean Sauce

Not to be confused with the dried black legumes used in Latin American cooking, Chinese black beans are actually soybeans that have been fermented in salt. Just a few black beans will add pungent, salty, complex notes to a dish, making them a great shortcut for working cooks. The beans are sold at Asian grocers and some supermarkets in bags, cans, or jars. They do not have to be refrigerated even after you open them if they are kept tightly wrapped or in a closed container. Serve with steamed short- or medium-grain rice.

Combine the black beans, soy sauce, vinegar, wine, garlic, ginger, and oil in a small bowl.

Lightly grease with vegetable oil an 8- or 9-inch square heat-proof glass baking dish and place the fish in the middle of the dish. Fold under any thin portions of fillet to make the fish even in thickness. Season lightly with salt. Place the asparagus around the fish. Drizzle the fish and asparagus with the sauce, then add 2 tablespoons water.

Wrap tightly with plastic wrap and cook in the microwave for 2 to 3 minutes on high power. (If your microwave is very powerful, you may want to check the fish after 1 minute.) Stir the asparagus, then continue cooking until the fish flakes and the asparagus is cooked through, 1 to 3 minutes more. Serve at once.

NOTE: When asparagus is out of season, look for broccolini, which is a cross between Chinese broccoli and asparagus.

PER SERVING: 205 calories,
30 g protein, 6 g carbohydrate,
6 g fat (1 g saturated),
58 mg cholesterol,
613 mg sodium, 1 g fiber

35 minutes

Serves 4

- 1 tablespoon unsalted butter
- 1 shallot, minced
- 8 ounces orzo or semi di melone pasta (see page 34)
- 3 cups low-sodium chicken broth
- 1/2 teaspoon salt, plus more to taste
- Pinch of saffron
- 4 skinless swordfish or tuna fillets, 6 ounces each and 1 inch thick
- Freshly ground pepper to taste

CHARMOULA

- 3 tablespoons chopped fresh Italian (flat-leaf) parsley
- 1/4 cup fresh lemon juice (from about 2 lemons)
- 1/2 to 1 teaspoon cayenne
- 1/2 teaspoon ground cumin
- 1/4 cup extra virgin olive oil

PER SERVING: 542 calories, 41 g protein, 48 g carbohydrate, 21 g fat (4 g saturated), 65 mg cholesterol, 845 mg sodium, 3 g fiber

Broiled Swordfish with Saffron Orzo & Charmoula

In this delicious dish, meaty swordfish sits atop a bed of buttery saffron orzo. But what really gives this meal zing is a drizzle of charmoula, a traditional Middle Eastern condiment. Cumin and a dash of cayenne in the sauce provide smoky heat, while lemon juice and parsley make the flaky fish taste fresh and light. Firmer fish like Pacific swordfish and tuna are best in this recipe, but mahi mahi, sea bass, or halibut fillets are good, too. Reduce the broiling time if you are using thinner fillets. (See photo on page 96.)

Preheat the broiler, placing the rack about 4 inches from the heating element. Line a baking sheet with foil and brush lightly with olive oil.

Melt the butter in a sauté pan over medium heat. Add the shallot and sauté about 2 minutes. Add the orzo and stir to coat with butter. Add the broth and 1/2 teaspoon salt. Bring to a boil, then stir in the saffron. Cover and simmer until the orzo is al dente, about 10 minutes.

While the orzo simmers, season the fish on both sides with salt and pepper. Arrange the fillets on the baking sheet and broil 4 minutes, then turn and broil until flaky, about 2 to 4 minutes more.

While the fish is cooking, make the charmoula: combine the parsley, lemon juice, cayenne, and cumin in a serving bowl. Stir in the olive oil and season with salt.

Place the fish on serving plates on a bed of saffron orzo, drizzle with the charmoula, and serve.

[**NOTE:** Pacific swordfish is a more sustainable choice than Atlantic.]

Halibut with Potatoes & Caper Sauce

Most of the ingredients for this caper sauce—capers, cornichons or other pickles, and olive oil—can be found in the pantry. Based on the French sauce ravigote, the sauce is chunky yet becomes creamy as you whisk in the hard-cooked egg yolks. Serve the sauce at room temperature to provide a nice contrast to the hot fish.

Preheat the broiler, placing the rack about 4 inches from the heating element.

Place the eggs in a small saucepan and add water to cover by 1 inch. Bring to a rolling boil and cook for 8 minutes. Remove from the heat, drain, and let cool under running water for a few minutes. When cool, peel and dice fine.

Meanwhile, place the potatoes in a saucepan and add water to cover by 1 inch. Season the water well with salt, cover, and bring to a boil. Reduce the heat to a simmer and cook, uncovered, until tender, about 15 minutes. Drain well.

Lightly oil a baking sheet, then place the halibut fillets on top, folding under any thin parts of the fillets to prevent them from overcooking. Season the fish well with salt and pepper. Broil until flaky, 4 to 5 minutes. Tent with foil and set aside to rest.

Combine the eggs, capers, cornichons, parsley, olive oil, and lemon juice in a bowl. Whisk well so that the egg yolks begin to break down and make the sauce creamy. Season with salt and pepper.

Spoon the sauce over the fish and the potatoes on serving plates, garnish with lemon wedges, and serve.

> **NOTE:** Cornichons are tiny, lightly sweet-and-sour French pickles available at delis and specialty markets. If they're not available, you can substitute your favorite mildly flavored pickle.

40 minutes
Serves 4

- 2 large eggs
- 8 ounces baby potatoes, halved if larger than 2 inches in diameter
- 4 halibut fillets, 6 to 7 ounces each
- Salt and freshly ground pepper to taste
- 2 tablespoons capers, drained and coarsely chopped
- ¼ cup chopped cornichon pickles
- ⅓ cup chopped fresh Italian (flat-leaf) parsley
- ¼ cup extra virgin olive oil
- 1 tablespoon fresh lemon juice, plus lemon wedges for garnish (about 1 lemon)

PER SERVING: 427 calories, 41 g protein, 7 g carbohydrate, 20 g fat (4 g saturated), 160 mg cholesterol, 413 mg sodium, 1 g fiber

20 minutes

Serves 4

6 tablespoons
unsalted butter

1½ tablespoons
drained capers

4 skinless petrale sole
fillets, about 6 ounces
each

Salt and freshly
ground pepper
to taste

1½ cups all-purpose flour

¼ cup vegetable oil

1 pound chopped
broccoli florets,
or 1 bunch asparagus
spears, chopped
into 1½-inch pieces

Fresh lemon juice
to taste

Sole with Broccoli & Caper Brown Butter

This dish is based on a classic French preparation of fish dipped in flour, fried, and served with beurre meunière, or brown butter flavored with lemon juice. Though the dish is simple to prepare, it's important to cook the butter at the correct temperature: it must be hot enough to brown but not so hot that it burns. As soon as you notice a nutty fragrance, it's time to take the butter off the heat.

Melt the butter in a small, heavy saucepan over medium-low heat and cook until it reaches a deep amber color and has a nutty fragrance. Reduce the temperature if necessary to prevent the butter from burning. Remove from the heat immediately and stir in the capers. Season with salt.

Meanwhile, pat the fish dry and season with salt and pepper. Place the flour in a shallow dish and dredge the fish in the flour, shaking off the excess.

Heat a large frying pan over medium heat, then add the oil. When the oil is very hot, add two fillets and cook until browned, 1 to 3 minutes per side, depending on the fillets' thickness. Remove with a slotted spatula and keep warm while you cook the remaining fillets.

While you're cooking the fish, steam the broccoli or asparagus until crisp-tender, 3 to 5 minutes.

To serve, distribute the fish and broccoli among serving plates. Drizzle each fillet with a little bit of lemon juice and season the broccoli with salt and pepper. Drizzle the caper brown butter over the fish and broccoli and serve.

[**NOTE:** If petrale sole isn't available, try English sole, flounder, cod, or whole sand dabs. Imported Dover sole is the classic choice for this dish, but it's not widely available.]

PER SERVING: 543 calories,
38 g protein, 24 g carbohydrate,
34 g fat (12 g saturated),
128 mg cholesterol,
237 mg sodium, 4 g fiber

25 minutes

Serves 4

- 2 tablespoons peanut or other vegetable oil
- 2 tablespoons unseasoned rice vinegar
- 4 teaspoons Asian sesame oil
- 4 teaspoons soy sauce
- ¼ cup minced fresh ginger
- 4 skinless white fish fillets such as cod, 6 to 8 ounces each and ½ inch thick

  Salt to taste
- 3 large green onions, thinly sliced

Ginger-Steamed Fish

In China, fish is traditionally steamed on a plate. This variation on the Chinese classic uses individual foil trays tucked into the steamer, allowing you to cook several fillets at the same time. If you like, cook some broccoli or asparagus in the steamer while you prepare the fish packets. Be sure to season the fish well with salt; otherwise, this dish may seem bland. Serve with short- or medium-grain rice.

Whisk together the vegetable oil, vinegar, sesame oil, and soy sauce in a small bowl. Stir in the ginger and set aside.

Tear off 4 pieces of foil, each about 12 by 6 inches. Place a fish fillet on each piece of foil. Turn up the edges of the foil to create a rim around the fish, so that each fillet is in a tray that won't allow liquids to get out but is still open on top.

Season each fillet evenly with salt. Spoon equal parts of the soy sauce mixture on each fillet. Sprinkle the green onions on top.

Set up a large bamboo or metal-mesh steamer and place 2 or 3 packages inside. Cover and steam until flaky, 6 to 8 minutes, depending on the thickness of the fish. Remove the packages carefully, reserving the cooking juices, and keep warm while you repeat with the remaining fillets.

Drizzle each fillet with the juices from its package and serve at once.

PER SERVING: 550 calories, 45 g protein, 57 g carbohydrate, 14 g fat (2 g saturated), 117 mg cholesterol, 480 mg sodium, 1 g fiber

TIP: You will need foil and a large steamer for this recipe. Alternatively, you can use the steaming method described for the Microwave-Steamed Sea Bass with Asparagus & Black Bean Sauce (page 106), cooking half of the fish at a time.

Snapper en Papillote with Cilantro & Tomatoes

35 minutes

Serves 4

I first had a version of this dish during my honeymoon, at a snack shack on the beach in Puerto Angel, a fishing village on the coast of Oaxaca, Mexico. Our waiter led us to a table under a thatched roof just 10 feet shy of the water. We had snapper prepared two ways: One in the traditional al mojo de ajo style, fried in butter and garlic, and the other enclosed in a foil packet with cilantro and thin wedges of tomato and onion. The just-tender vegetables and buttery fish settled in a rich broth with a hint of citrus.

Preheat the oven to 450°F.

Place the potatoes in a saucepan and add just enough water to cover. Season the water liberally with salt, cover, and bring to a boil. Reduce the heat to a simmer and cook until the potatoes are tender when pierced with a knife, 12 to 15 minutes.

Meanwhile, tear off 4 large pieces of foil, each about 12 by 16 inches, and place on the counter. Rub some of the butter on each piece of foil, leaving a 1-inch border around the edges, then chop the rest of the 2 tablespoons butter into small pieces.

Using half of the onions, cilantro, and tomato, divide the vegetables evenly among the foil pieces, arranging them on one half of each foil piece. Top each pile of vegetables with a fillet of fish. Season the fish with salt and pepper, then drizzle with the lemon juice and wine. Layer the remaining onions, cilantro, and tomatoes evenly on top of the fish, then dot with the butter pieces.

For each packet, fold the clean half of the foil over the fish, then, starting at one corner, fold and crimp the edges to seal tightly. Place the packages on a large baking sheet and bake until the fish flakes, 17 to 20 minutes.

When the potatoes are done, toss with the remaining 1 to 2 tablespoons butter, a pinch of salt, and some freshly ground pepper. Keep warm.

Carefully unwrap or cut open the foil packages with a pair of scissors, being careful not to burn yourself on the hot steam that is released. To serve, divide the potatoes among serving plates, then transfer the fish and vegetables to the plates and top with the juices.

8 to 12 small new potatoes

2 tablespoons unsalted butter, plus 1 to 2 tablespoons for tossing

½ onion, thinly sliced

Handful of fresh cilantro, thick stems removed

1 tomato, thinly sliced

4 skinless red snapper fillets, about 6 ounces each

Salt and freshly ground pepper to taste

3 tablespoons fresh lemon juice (from about 1 lemon)

Dry white wine or white wine vinegar for drizzling

TIP: Instead of traditional parchment paper, this recipe uses aluminum foil, which is a little easier to work with and more widely available, but you can use parchment paper if you like.

PER SERVING: 291 calories, 26 g protein, 24 g carbohydrate, 10 g fat (6 g saturated), 65 mg cholesterol, 59 mg sodium, 2 g fiber

30 minutes

Serves 4

3 to 4 tablespoons
        unsalted butter

4 cloves garlic,
   thinly sliced

1 leek, cleaned
   and thinly sliced
   (see Tip, page 99)

1 small fennel bulb,
   quartered, cored,
   and very thinly sliced
   (see Tip, page 121)

4 pounds mussels,
   scrubbed and
   debearded right
   before cooking

2 cups Vouvray
   or a light-bodied
   sauvignon blanc, or
   other dry white wine

1 bay leaf

1 sprig fresh thyme

1 tablespoon minced
   fresh Italian (flat-leaf)
   parsley

   Salt and freshly
   ground pepper
   to taste

Steamed Mussels with Fennel & Leeks

This version of moules marinières, the popular French dish of steamed mussels, is wonderful made and served with a fruity but crisp white wine such as Vouvray from France's Loire Valley. The wine's flavor is imparted to the mussels as they steam, forming a good partnership with the pleasantly astringent fennel. Serve with a baguette and salad.

Heat 1 tablespoon of the butter in a large heavy stockpot or Dutch oven over medium heat. Add the garlic, leek, and fennel and sauté, stirring occasionally, until just softened, 2 to 3 minutes.

Add the mussels, wine, bay leaf, and thyme to the stockpot. Increase the heat to high, cover the pot, and bring the liquid to a boil. Reduce the heat to medium and continue steaming, shaking the pot once or twice, until the mussels open, 3 to 5 minutes.

Remove the mussels with a slotted spoon, transferring them either to one large serving bowl or individual serving bowls. Keep warm while you cook the liquid remaining in the pot, uncovered, stirring once or twice, until slightly reduced, 2 to 4 minutes. Remove from the heat and stir in the remaining 2 to 3 tablespoons butter and the parsley. Add salt and pepper to taste, and then pour the sauce over mussels. Serve at once.

NOTE: Mussels are inexpensive and take only minutes to cook, but they need special care. Buy the freshest ones you can find and use them the day you buy them, or hold them overnight in the refrigerator in a bowl inside a larger bowl of ice, covered with a damp towel (they need to breathe). Discard any uncooked mussels with open shells that won't close with a gentle squeeze. Farmed mussels generally have less grit and don't have the barnacles that need to be scrubbed off of wild ones.

PER SERVING: 582 calories,
56 g protein, 26 g carbohydrate,
19 g fat (8 g saturated),
150 mg cholesterol,
1,340 mg sodium, 2 g fiber

2 pounds Yukon gold potatoes, peeled and halved, or quartered if large

Salt to taste

5 ounces wasabi peas

4 skinless fillets of red snapper, sole, or other thin white fish, 5 to 6 ounces each

2 to 3 tablespoons unsalted butter

Freshly ground pepper to taste

¼ cup hot low-fat milk or potato cooking water, plus more as needed

Vegetable oil for sautéing

Wasabi Pea–Crusted Fish with Mashed Yukon Golds

It's hard not to become addicted to wasabi peas, those crunchy, spicy Japanese snacks that are sold in Asian grocery stores, health food stores, specialty markets, and even drugstores. That's why I was so excited when I first heard about sautéing fish with a crust made of crushed wasabi peas. The fish doesn't have the same intensity as the sinus-clearing snacks, but the wasabi crumbs create a crunchy coating with a hint of horseradish flavor as well as sweetness and nuttiness from the dried peas. You could serve the fish with any type of mashed potato, but Yukon golds have an appealing yellow color and so much natural flavor that they don't need much butter or cream. (See photo on page 97.)

Place the potatoes in a saucepan, add water to cover by 1 to 2 inches, and season well with salt. Cover and bring to a boil then reduce to a simmer; cook until tender when pierced with a knife, 12 to 15 minutes, depending on their size. Drain well, reserving about ½ cup of the potato cooking water, if using, then return the potatoes to the saucepan.

Meanwhile, place the peas in a large, heavy-duty resealable bag. Spread the peas out in a flat layer, press the air out of the bag, and seal the bag. Crush with a heavy cast-iron pot, rolling pin, or mallet until the peas have been reduced to a powder and small pieces.

Spread out about two-thirds of the peas on a large plate. Season the fish with salt on both sides, then press into the wasabi pea crumbs. Pour the extra pea crumbs on top, and press firmly until the fish is coated well on both sides, especially with the powder. There will be some crushed peas left over.

Add the butter, salt, and pepper to the potatoes; mash, adding a little bit of the milk or water at a time. Cover and keep warm.

Heat a large frying pan over medium-high heat. When the pan is quite hot, add enough oil to coat the bottom of the pan. When the oil is hot, add 2 or 3 fillets and cook until browned, 2 to 3 minutes. Flip carefully, then cook until the other side is browned and the fish is cooked through, about 2 more minutes. Repeat with the remaining fillets and serve with the mashed potatoes.

PER SERVING: 446 calories, 36 g protein, 52 g carbohydrate, 10 g fat (4 g saturated), 69 mg cholesterol, 231 mg sodium, 5 g fiber

TIP: Using fairly high heat ensures that the fish cooks through quickly, before it has a chance to dry out, while the crust becomes amazingly crisp and lightly browned. Try not to handle the potatoes too much; the more you mix them, the more gluten is released, resulting in a gluey texture.

Pecan-Crusted Trout & Parsley Rice Pilaf

An easy way to get a crispy coating on trout is to sprinkle it with ground nuts and bread crumbs, dot it with a little butter, and bake it in a hot oven. The crusted fish cries out for a little lemon, and it sits atop a bed of parsley rice pilaf. Served with a salad or Stir-fried Greens (see page 162) the trout makes a quick and elegant meal for company. You need a food processor to prepare this dish.

Preheat the oven to 450°F. Line a baking sheet with aluminum foil and grease lightly with butter.

Heat the olive oil in a saucepan over medium heat. Add the onion and sauté until tender, about 8 minutes. Increase heat to high, add the rice, and stir until all the grains are coated evenly with the oil, 1 to 2 minutes. Add 1½ cups water, 1 teaspoon salt, and pepper. Stir to combine and bring to a boil. Reduce the heat to low or medium-low and simmer, covered, until the rice is tender, about 18 minutes.

As the rice pilaf is cooking, place the pecans in a food processor and pulse until the nuts are finely ground but not oily. Add the bread crumbs and pulse briefly to combine. Cut each trout into two fillets, then place skin side down on the prepared baking sheet. Season the flesh with salt and pepper, sprinkle with the pecan mixture, then dot with the butter. Place in the oven and bake until the edges of the skin are crisp and the thick part of the flesh is opaque, 5 to 8 minutes.

Increase the heat to broil and place the pan near the heating element for a few minutes until the topping is golden brown (watch carefully, as the nuts will burn easily).

As the fish is cooking, cut the stems off the parsley right where they meet the leaves, then finely chop the leaves in the food processor. When the rice is done, remove from the heat, quickly stir in the parsley, cover, and let stand 5 minutes before serving.

Arrange the trout fillets on a bed of pilaf on serving plates and serve with the lemon wedges.

TIP: When making rice pilaf it's important to coat the rice grains well with oil on high heat before adding the liquid. Then, keep the heat as low as possible while still maintaining a gentle simmer. You should see a small amount of steam escape from the pot (try not to open the pot to sneak a peek).

35 minutes
Serves 4

- 1½ tablespoons olive oil
- 1 cup chopped onion
- 1 cup long-grain white rice
- 1 teaspoon salt, plus more to taste
- Freshly ground pepper to taste
- ½ cup pecan pieces
- 3 tablespoons dried bread crumbs
- 2 butterflied whole rainbow trout, heads and tails removed (1 to 1½ pounds total)
- 1½ tablespoons cold unsalted butter, cut into small pieces
- ½ bunch fresh Italian (flat-leaf) parsley
- 1 lemon, cut into wedges

PER SERVING: 499 calories, 21 g protein, 52 g carbohydrate, 23 g fat (5 g saturated), 55 mg cholesterol, 675 mg sodium, 3 g fiber

Determining When Chicken Is Done

To determine whether a chicken breast is cooked properly, press the top of the thickest part with your finger. It should feel quite firm but not rubbery. If you cut into it, the interior should no longer be pink. To be absolutely sure, insert an instant-read thermometer into the thickest portion of the breast; it should read 165°F. Let the cooked chicken rest, tented with foil, for a few minutes before serving, during which time the temperature will rise another few degrees.

Chicken and Turkey

Boneless, skinless chicken breasts have become almost a food group unto themselves. They are easy to prepare, low in fat and cholesterol, and serve as a blank slate for flavors from almost any culinary tradition.

Unfortunately, their flavor can also be pretty underwhelming. Stripped of bone and skin, the lean pieces of chicken dry out easily. Pan-frying chicken breasts can be particularly challenging. Ideally, you'd like them to be golden brown on the outside and juicy on the inside. More often than not, you end up with either a nicely browned hockey puck or a juicy piece of meat with alarming traces of pink inside. The best approach is to use small, thin half breasts around 6 ounces each, quickly browning them over moderately high heat in a sauté pan before finishing them in a 400 or 450°F oven.

Though this chapter provides lots of options for preparing chicken breasts, you'll also discover recipes using turkey breast, ground turkey, and poultry sausage for variety. You can also try substituting turkey breast cutlets for chicken breasts in these recipes. Simply adjust the cooking time if they are thinner or thicker than typical chicken breasts.

Facing page: Chicken with Rajas & Spanish Rice (recipe on page 124). Turkey Burgers with Green Chiles (recipe on page 133)

119

2 bunches Swiss chard
or other winter greens

2 teaspoons extra virgin
olive oil

2 cloves garlic, minced

½ cup low-sodium
chicken broth

2 teaspoons sherry
vinegar or red wine
vinegar

Salt and freshly
ground pepper
to taste

4 small boneless,
skinless chicken
half breasts,
4 to 5 ounces each

2 to 3 tablespoons
vegetable oil

Pan-Fried Chicken Breasts with Braised Winter Greens

With nutritious, flavor-packed greens and small, tender pan-fried breasts, this dish is the ultimate quick meal for poultry lovers. The juices from the greens add moisture to the chicken. To speed up the recipe, use pre-washed and chopped winter greens. Serve with boiled new potatoes or the Sweet Potato Fries (page 122).

Remove the stems from the greens, then chop the leaves crosswise into 1-inch ribbons.

Heat the olive oil in a sauté pan over low heat. Add the garlic and sauté until fragrant, about 30 seconds. Add the greens and increase the heat to medium. Stir until the greens start to wilt. Add the broth and bring to a simmer. Cover and cook until the greens are tender, about 5 minutes for chard, 10 minutes for heartier greens like kale. Stir in the vinegar, taste, and season with salt and pepper. Keep warm.

Meanwhile, season each breast liberally with salt and pepper.

Heat a large frying pan over medium-high heat. Add 2 tablespoons of the vegetable oil and heat until almost smoking. Carefully add two of the half breasts. Sauté until browned and the inside has no trace of pink but is still juicy, about 5 minutes per side. Remove with a slotted spoon to a warm plate and repeat with remaining half breasts.

Divide the greens among four serving plates. Top with the chicken, drizzle with pan juices, and serve.

PER SERVING: 215 calories,
27 g protein, 2 g carbohydrate,
11 g fat (2 g saturated),
65 mg cholesterol, 211 mg sodium,
0 g fiber

TIP: If the chicken half breasts are larger than 5 ounces each, sear them first, then finish them in a 400°F oven, as instructed in the recipe for Pan-Roasted Chicken with Coriander Vegetables (page 121). For more on searing, see page 15.

Pan-Roasted Chicken with Coriander Vegetables

40 minutes

Serves 4

Simplicity is key to this dish. The coriander-scented fennel, carrot, and red onion contribute sweet and astringent flavors and a colorful backdrop to a simple chicken breast, which is moistened with a quick pan sauce. For a side dish, steam some long-grain rice while you prepare the chicken.

Preheat the oven to 400°F.

Season the chicken breasts with salt and pepper on both sides.

Heat a large sauté pan over medium-high heat. When it's very hot, add the oil. When the oil is very hot, add two of the chicken breasts. Sear on one side for 1 to 2 minutes, then place browned side up on a baking sheet. Repeat with the remaining chicken. Roast the chicken in the oven until cooked through, about 12 minutes.

While the chicken is roasting, discard all but 1½ tablespoons of the oil in the pan and place the pan over medium heat. Add the coriander and onion and cook, stirring often, for about 5 minutes. Stir in the fennel, carrot, and bay leaf. Add the wine, increase the heat to high, and deglaze the pan, stirring to scrape up any bits that may have stuck to the bottom. Add the broth and bring to a simmer. Keep at a steady simmer until the vegetables are crisp-tender, 3 to 5 minutes. Season with salt and pepper.

To serve, use a slotted spoon to divide the vegetables among four serving plates and top each with a chicken breast. Whisk the butter into the sauce and drizzle it over the vegetables and chicken.

4	boneless, skinless chicken half breasts, about 6 ounces each
	Salt and freshly ground pepper to taste
2	tablespoons olive oil
1	teaspoon ground coriander
¼	red onion, thinly sliced
1	fennel bulb, thinly sliced
1	carrot, peeled and julienned (see Tip, page 24)
1	bay leaf
½	cup dry white wine
½	cup low-sodium chicken broth
1	tablespoon unsalted butter

TIP: To thinly slice fennel, cut it into quarters through the core. Cut out the core from each wedge with a diagonal cut, then thinly slice each of the quarters with a sharp chef's knife.

PER SERVING: 300 calories, 29 g protein, 7 g carbohydrate, 15 g fat (4 g saturated), 76 mg cholesterol, 138 mg sodium, 2 g fiber

35 minutes

Serves 4

1½ tablespoons
   vegetable oil

2 pounds unpeeled
   jewel or orange-
   skinned sweet
   potatoes

2 to 2½ teaspoons
   seasoning salt

4 sprigs fresh thyme
   or rosemary
   (optional)

4 boneless, skinless
   chicken half breasts,
   about 6 ounces
   each

Chicken Breasts with Sweet Potato Fries

Sweet potatoes are available most of the year, but a lot of people wonder what to do with them when it's not Thanksgiving or Christmas. Baked whole like a russet potato, sweet potatoes have so much moisture and flavor that they need almost no butter or salt. I also like to cut them into wedges and roast them to make oven fries. Sweet potatoes have more moisture and sugar than regular potatoes and don't take as long to cook (they also burn easily). To help the wedges develop a brown, crisp crust, make sure the pan is evenly coated with oil and close to the heating element in your oven. Serve with a green salad or steamed green vegetables.

Preheat the oven to 425°F and place a rack in the bottom third of the oven close to the heating element. Coat a large, heavy-duty baking sheet with vegetable oil.

Cut the potatoes in half width-wise (not length-wise), then cut each half into triangular wedges about ½ inch thick at the widest point. Toss with 1 tablespoon oil and ½ teaspoon seasoning salt. Spread in a single layer on the baking sheet, then sprinkle with a little more seasoning salt to taste (the intensity of the flavor will vary depending on the brand). Drape the herb sprigs, if using them, on top of the potato wedges.

Roast the potatoes until browned on the bottom, 12 to 15 minutes, then turn the potatoes and roast until tender, golden brown, and blistered, 12 to 15 minutes more. Watch carefully to prevent them from burning. Discard the herbs, or reserve them to use as a garnish.

While the potatoes are cooking, season the chicken with the remaining 1½ to 2 teaspoons seasoning salt. Heat the remaining ½ tablespoon oil in a large ovenproof nonstick frying pan over medium-high heat. Add the chicken and sauté until browned, about 5 minutes, then turn the chicken over and sauté for a few minutes more. Transfer the pan to the oven and roast until the chicken is cooked through, about 12 minutes.

Remove the chicken from the oven and let rest for a few minutes before serving with the sweet potatoes, garnished with the reserved herb sprigs, if you like.

PER SERVING: 405 calories,
42 g protein, 40 g carbohydrate,
7 g fat (1 g saturated),
99 mg cholesterol,
905 mg sodium, 4 g fiber

TIP: Draping the sweet potatoes with thyme or rosemary branches infuses them with flavor and fragrance and eliminates the need to chop the herbs.

35 minutes

Serves 4

- 1 package Mexican- or Spanish-style rice mix (serving 4)
- 8 ounces poblano or Anaheim chiles
- 4 boneless, skinless chicken half breasts, about 6 ounces each

  Salt and freshly ground pepper to taste
- 1 tablespoon vegetable oil
- 1 large onion, sliced

Chicken with Rajas & Spanish Rice

I first had chicken breast with rajas, or roasted chile pepper strips, at a Mexican restaurant near my home in San Francisco. It was so good, yet so simple, that I knew I wanted to re-create it at home. The rajas take a little while to prepare, because you have to char and peel the peppers, so I serve them with an instant rice mix to speed things up. The poblano and Anaheim peppers have a wonderfully complex and fruity flavor. Though they are a little spicy, the sweet browned onions temper their heat. (See photo on page 118.)

Preheat the oven to 425°F. Prepare the rice mix according to the package directions. Let it rest off the heat when it's done.

As the rice is cooking, blacken the peppers (see Tip below). This should take about 10 minutes over a gas flame. Seal the peppers in a plastic bag for a few minutes to let them cool in their own steam (this will make the peppers easier to peel).

Season the chicken with salt and pepper. Heat a large frying pan over medium-high heat. Add the oil. When the oil shimmers, add the chicken. Sear on one side until very brown, about 5 minutes. Turn the chicken and brown for a few minutes more. Transfer the chicken to a baking sheet and place in the oven. Roast until the chicken is no longer pink in the center, about 12 minutes.

Return the pan to the heat, add the onion, and cook until slightly browned, 1 to 2 minutes. Reduce the heat to medium and cook until tender, about 8 minutes.

Cut open the peppers and scrape out the seeds and membrane. Cut the peppers into long strips slightly thinner than ¼ inch thick. When the onion is done, stir in the peppers and season with salt and pepper. Serve the chicken with the rajas and rice.

PER SERVING: 360 calories, 43 g protein, 28 g carbohydrate, 8 g fat (1 g saturated), 99 mg cholesterol, 277 mg sodium, 3 g fiber

TIP: To blacken peppers, hold them with tongs or place them on a grate over a medium flame; place them on a baking sheet under a pre-heated broiler; or use a grill pan over high heat. In each case, turn the peppers frequently as they blacken and blister; it's not necessary to char every inch of skin.

Mustard-Crusted Chicken with Mango Raita

This recipe goes out on a limb with unusual flavors and textures to make those everyday chicken breasts a little more interesting. The chicken is coated with sweet mustard and brown mustard seeds, which pop under the broiler and become a toasty, crunchy coating. The mango raita is a creamy Indian yogurt relish, which is both cooling and mildly spicy at the same time, with minced red onion, fiery jalapeño, and chunks of sweet mango. Raita often contains toasted mustard seeds, so it's a good match for the chicken. Serve with basmati rice.

Preheat the broiler, placing the rack about 4 inches from the heating element.

Season each piece of chicken with about ⅛ teaspoon salt, season with pepper, and then brush on both sides with the mustard.

Place the mustard seeds in a shallow dish. Press one side of each piece of chicken into the seeds to coat evenly.

Broil the chicken, seed side down, for 5 minutes. Turn the pieces over and continue broiling until the chicken is no longer pink in the middle, about 5 minutes. The seeds will pop as the chicken broils; if they start to burn, turn the chicken over again to finish cooking.

While the chicken is cooking, stir together all the raita ingredients in a bowl. Serve the hot chicken with the raita.

[
NOTE: Whole brown mustard seeds are available in Indian markets and in the spice section of many supermarkets.
]

30 minutes

Serves 4

CHICKEN

4 boneless, skinless chicken half breasts, about 6 ounces each

½ teaspoon salt

Freshly ground pepper to taste

2 to 3 tablespoons sweet-hot mustard, or a mixture of honey and mustard

2 to 3 tablespoons whole brown mustard seeds

RAITA

1½ cups nonfat or low-fat plain yogurt

Pinch of ground cumin

½ cup minced red onion

1 ripe mango, peeled, seeded, and diced (see Tip, page 103)

¼ bunch chives, chopped, or 2 to 3 chopped green onions, green part only

1 jalapeño chile, seeded and minced (see Tip, page 26)

¼ teaspoon salt, plus more to taste

Freshly ground pepper to taste

PER SERVING: 317 calories, 47 g protein, 21 g carbohydrate, 3 g fat (1 g saturated), 100 mg cholesterol, 738 mg sodium, 3 g fiber

30 minutes

Serves 4

2 large eggs

1½ cups panko (see Note)

4 boneless, skinless chicken half breasts, about 6 ounces each

4 large slices prosciutto (about 4 ounces)

3 ounces herbed fresh goat cheese

Salt and freshly ground pepper to taste

¼ cup olive oil or vegetable oil

2 cloves garlic, sliced

20 ounces pre-washed spinach

1 tablespoon fresh lemon juice and lemon wedges for serving (about 1 lemon total)

PER SERVING: 403 calories, 57 g protein, 15 g carbohydrate, 13 g fat (6 g saturated), 223 mg cholesterol, 668 mg sodium, 5 g fiber

Goat Cheese–Stuffed Chicken Breasts with Spinach

Since chicken breasts dry out easily, it's a good idea to stuff them with ingredients that add moisture and flavor. In this recipe herbed fresh goat cheese and prosciutto are tucked into a little pocket cut into each breast before the chicken is fried with a crisp bread crumb coating. Serve with thick slices of crusty sourdough bread.

Preheat the oven to 450°F.

Whisk the eggs lightly in a shallow bowl. Place the bread crumbs in another shallow bowl or on a plate.

With a sharp knife, carefully cut horizontally about halfway into one breast to create a large pocket about the length and width of the breast. If possible, try to leave the ends uncut so the stuffing doesn't fall out.

Layer a folded piece of prosciutto along the insides of the pocket, then spread one quarter of the goat cheese over the prosciutto. Carefully close the opening and seal with a toothpick, if desired. Season the chicken with salt and pepper. Repeat with the remaining breasts.

Dip each breast completely into the egg, allow the excess egg to drip off, then dip into the bread crumbs. Pack the bread crumbs on to cover completely, then shake off any excess.

Heat the oil in a large frying pan (or use more oil and two pans) over medium-high heat until very hot. Carefully place the chicken in the oil and fry until golden brown, 2 to 3 minutes per side.

Transfer the chicken to a baking sheet and bake in the oven until the chicken is cooked through, about 10 minutes.

While the chicken is baking, remove and discard all but about 1 tablespoon of the oil from the frying pan used for the chicken, leaving the brown crispy bits in the pan. Return the pan to medium heat and add the garlic. Sauté briefly, scraping up any browned bits from the bottom of the pan. Add the spinach, a little at a time, stirring until it wilts. Season with salt and pepper. Add the lemon juice.

Divide the spinach mixture among 4 serving plates. Arrange the breasts over the spinach, garnish with the lemon wedges, and serve.

NOTE: Panko, or Japanese bread crumbs, is available in the Asian food sections in some grocery stores and in Asian markets. You can substitute regular packaged or fresh bread crumbs.

35 minutes

Serves 4

- 2 1-inch pieces fresh ginger, one peeled and finely minced or grated (see Tip, page 30), plus one unpeeled and sliced
- ¼ cup soy sauce
- ¼ cup Chinese rice wine or dry sherry
- 1 teaspoon red chile-garlic sauce
- ¼ teaspoon Asian sesame oil

  Pinch of sugar
- 1½ pounds boneless, skinless chicken breast or leg meat, cut thinly into bite-size pieces
- 2 tablespoons vegetable oil
- 1 large shallot, minced
- 1 pound thin asparagus, trimmed and cut into 2-inch pieces
- 2 teaspoons cornstarch mixed with 3 tablespoons water
- 2 teaspoons sesame seeds

PER SERVING: 297 calories, 42 g protein, 8 g carbohydrate, 10 g fat (1 g saturated), 99 mg cholesterol, 352 mg sodium, 3 g fiber. The calories and other nutrients absorbed from marinades vary and are difficult to estimate, so the marinade is not included in this analysis.

Chicken-Asparagus Stir-Fry with Chile

In this recipe stir-fried chicken and asparagus are coated with a lightly spicy sauce. Use only as much cornstarch slurry as is needed to barely thicken the sauce. Substitute green beans when asparagus is out of season. Serve with steamed short- or medium-grain rice.

Combine the minced ginger, soy sauce, rice wine, chile sauce, sesame oil, and sugar. Place the chicken in a bowl, then add enough of the marinade to just coat, reserving the extra sauce. Set the chicken aside while you prepare the vegetables.

Heat 1 tablespoon of the vegetable oil in a wok or large frying pan over medium-high heat. Add half of the sliced ginger and shallot and stir-fry briefly, until fragrant. Add the asparagus and stir-fry for a minute or two. Add a few tablespoons of water. Cover, reduce the heat to medium-low and cook until the asparagus is crisp-tender, 2 to 3 minutes. Remove the asparagus from the wok and set aside, draining any excess water from the asparagus.

Increase the heat to high and add the remaining 1 tablespoon oil to the wok. Add the remaining ginger and shallot and stir-fry briefly, until fragrant. Add the chicken and stir-fry until browned on all sides and no longer pink in the center, about 5 minutes.

Return the asparagus to the pan with ¼ cup of the reserved sauce. Bring to a simmer and cook for a minute or two. Stir in just enough of the cornstarch mixture (slurry) to create a light sauce that just coats the chicken and asparagus. Add a little at a time while simmering and give it a few seconds to thicken after each addition. Remove the wok from the heat, discard the ginger, and sprinkle with the sesame seeds before serving.

Noel's Chicken Adobo

This delicious but quick version of Philippine adobo was created by my friend Noel Advincula. The combination of soy sauce and vinegar provides the traditional tangy edge to the sauce, while coconut milk adds richness and complexity. This is also good made with boneless, skinless chicken legs. Serve over steamed rice.

In a deep nonstick pan, combine the chicken, garlic, shallot, black pepper, bay leaf, vinegar, chicken broth, and soy sauce. Bring to a simmer, cover and cook until the chicken is mostly cooked through, about 10 minutes.

Transfer the mixture to a bowl and remove the chicken pieces from the sauce.

Wipe out the pan, add the oil, and heat over medium-high heat. When the oil is hot, add the chicken and sauté for about 1½ minutes per side. Add the bell pepper and sauté until softened, about 3 minutes.

Return the sauce to the pan. Add the coconut milk and red pepper flakes and simmer until the sauce is heated through and the flavors blend, 3 to 5 minutes. Serve at once.

40 minutes

Serves 4

1½	pounds boneless, skinless chicken half breasts, each cut into 3 or 4 pieces
3	cloves garlic, minced
1	shallot, finely chopped
1	teaspoon coarsely ground black pepper
1	bay leaf
6	tablespoons red or white wine vinegar
½	cup low-sodium chicken broth
¼	cup reduced-sodium soy sauce
1	tablespoon vegetable oil
1	red bell pepper, cut into bite-size strips
1	cup coconut milk, can shaken before measuring
½ to 1	teaspoon red pepper flakes

PER SERVING: 385 calories, 42 g protein, 10 g carbohydrate, 20 g fat (12 g saturated), 101 mg cholesterol, 640 mg sodium, 2 g fiber

30 minutes

Serves 4

1½ pounds boneless, skinless chicken breasts, cut into about 20 two-inch pieces

Salt and freshly ground pepper to taste

1 tablespoon extra virgin olive oil

2 tablespoons fresh lemon juice (from about 1 lemon)

10 sprigs fresh rosemary, each about 8 inches long, or wooden skewers

2 large zucchini, cut in half lengthwise then cut into slices about 2 inches thick

20 large cherry or cocktail tomatoes

½ red onion, cut into large dice (optional)

PER SERVING: 225 calories, 41 g protein, 8 g carbohydrate, 3 g fat (1 g saturated), 99 mg cholesterol, 122 mg sodium, 2 g fiber.
The calories and other nutrients absorbed from marinades vary and are difficult to estimate, so the marinade is not included in this analysis.

Rosemary-Skewered Chicken with Zucchini

In this recipe, rosemary branches serve as skewers, infusing the chicken and zucchini chunks with their delicious scent and flavor. If you have your own rosemary plant, pick out large sprigs that seem strong enough to go through a piece of chicken but are not much thicker than wooden skewers. Regular wooden or metal skewers may work better than the flimsy rosemary sprigs available at most supermarkets (wooden skewers should be soaked for 30 minutes in water before grilling). Serve with warmed pita or couscous.

If you plan to use a grill, prepare a fire or preheat a gas grill for cooking over medium-high heat. You can also use a grill pan, placed over high heat, for this recipe.

Place the chicken in a shallow bowl, season with salt and pepper, then add the olive oil and lemon juice. Toss well and set aside to marinate while you prepare the vegetables.

Grasp the rosemary sprigs a few inches from the top, then use your other hand to pull off the needles below, leaving 2 to 3 inches of needles at the top. Thread a piece of chicken on the rosemary sprig or skewer, then follow with a piece of zucchini, a cherry tomato, and a piece of onion, if using. Repeat with the same ingredients, then go on to the next skewer.

Place on the grill or preheated grill pan and cook for about 5 minutes on one side, then flip and cook another 5 minutes. Continue cooking, turning the skewers to brown all sides, until the chicken is no longer pink in the center, 2 to 5 minutes more. Serve at once.

20 minutes

Serves 4

- 8 ounces arugula
- 1 jicama, peeled and cut into strips about 1 inch wide and thick (see Note, page 58)
- 2 tablespoons Italian vinaigrette dressing, or to taste
- 3 pieces soft, fresh lahvosh, about 8 by 14 inches each
- 8 ounces cream cheese, at room temperature
- 1½ pounds sliced roast turkey
- 1 14½-ounce can artichoke hearts or hearts of palm, thinly sliced

Turkey Aram Sandwiches with Hearts of Palm

This California version of a traditional Middle Eastern rolled sandwich is made with soft, fresh flatbread spread with cream cheese for moisture and then piled with turkey, arugula, crunchy jicama, and artichoke hearts or hearts of palm. Serve with soup for a light meal, or cut into smaller slices and serve as an appetizer. The sandwiches can be made a few hours ahead.

Heat the oven to 350°F.

Combine the arugula and jicama in a large bowl and toss with the vinaigrette.

Place the lahvosh directly on the oven racks for a minute or two until slightly toasted but not dried out; you will need to be able to roll it without cracking it.

Place a piece of lahvosh on a clean work surface. Evenly spread one-third of the cream cheese on top, leaving a 1-inch-wide border uncovered on one long end. Cover the cream cheese with one-third of the turkey, one-third of the arugula and jicama mixture, and one-third of the artichoke hearts or hearts of palm. Starting with the long side that doesn't have a border, begin rolling the bread up as tightly as you can until you have formed a long roll. Repeat with the remaining lahvosh, cream cheese, turkey, arugula, jicama, and artichoke hearts or hearts of palm.

At this point, you can wrap the roll tightly in plastic wrap and chill for a few hours before slicing. To serve immediately, cut each roll into 4 slices to serve as a main course (a main-course serving is 3 slices), or cut into 6 to 8 slices to serve as an appetizer. If you like, use toothpicks to hold each piece together. Arrange the pieces on a plate so you can see all the fillings and serve.

> **NOTE:** You can find packages of soft lahvosh—Middle Eastern flatbread—in health food stores, Middle Eastern markets, and some supermarkets. Don't mistake it for the dry, crackerlike bread that's also called flatbread. If you can't find lahvosh use large flour tortillas instead. You'll need about six.

PER SERVING: 599 calories, 57 g protein, 21 g carbohydrate, 33 g fat (16 g saturated), 183 mg cholesterol, 406 mg sodium, 10 g fiber

Turkey Burgers
with Green Chiles

For those who don't eat red meat but do crave a juicy burger every now and then, this is a delicious way to go. Though ground turkey has become popular as an alternative to beef for burgers, the two aren't entirely interchangeable. Ground turkey, especially ground turkey breast, is very lean, so it dries out easily. Turkey also doesn't have as much natural flavor as beef, which makes the spices, green chiles, and cheese in this dish especially welcome. The most important part is cooking the burgers just long enough so they're not a health risk (no longer pink in the center) but not so long that they become dried out. (See photo on page 119.)

Using your hands, thoroughly combine the turkey, salt, cumin, oregano, cayenne, and chiles. Shape into 4 patties about 1 inch thick.

Heat a lightly oiled nonstick grill pan or frying pan over medium-high heat. Add the patties and cook for 4 to 5 minutes. Flip the patties, top with a few slices of cheese, and cook until no longer pink in the middle, 4 to 5 minutes more.

Meanwhile, toast the bread. Spread with mayonnaise and top with the tomato. Sprinkle the tomato lightly with salt, add the burgers and lettuce, and serve.

25 minutes

Serves 4

1	pound lean ground turkey
½	teaspoon salt, plus more to taste
¼	teaspoon ground cumin
¼	teaspoon dried oregano, crumbled
¼	teaspoon cayenne
½	cup canned diced green chiles, drained
2 to 3	ounces Monterey Jack cheese, thinly sliced
8	slices sourdough sandwich bread
	Mayonnaise for serving
1	vine-ripened tomato, sliced
	Iceberg or other lettuce leaves for serving

PER SERVING: 357 calories, 29 g protein, 29 g carbohydrate, 14 g fat (5 g saturated), 97 mg cholesterol, 832 mg sodium, 2 g fiber

TIP: If you like, add some sliced avocado to the top of each burger.

3 tablespoons
fresh lemon juice
(from about 1 lemon)

¼ cup reduced-sodium
soy sauce

2 tablespoons rice wine
or dry sherry

½ teaspoon sugar

¼ teaspoon Asian
sesame oil

1 pound boneless,
skinless chicken
breasts, cut into
large dice

2 tablespoons
vegetable oil

3 cloves garlic, minced

1 2-inch piece unpeeled
fresh ginger, sliced

4 dried red chiles, sliced,
plus chiles for garnish

½ teaspoon finely
chopped lemon zest

1 onion, diced

8 ounces snow peas,
trimmed

2 teaspoons
cornstarch mixed with
2 tablespoons water

⅓ cup unsalted
roasted peanuts

PER SERVING: 350 calories,
33 g protein, 19 g carbohydrate,
15 g fat (2 g saturated),
66 mg cholesterol,
681 mg sodium, 5 mg fiber

Lemon Chicken Stir-Fry with Peanuts

This light and simple stir-fry gets a sweet and sour zing from the addition of lemon zest and lemon juice. Don't leave out the peanuts—they're a delicious touch. Serve with steamed short- or medium-grain rice.

Whisk together the lemon juice, soy sauce, wine, sugar, and sesame oil in a bowl until the sugar dissolves. Place the chicken in a separate bowl with 2 tablespoons of the sauce. Set aside to marinate while you prepare the vegetables.

Heat 1 tablespoon of the vegetable oil in a wok or large frying pan over medium-high heat. Add half of the garlic, ginger, and chiles and all of the lemon zest; stir-fry until fragrant, about 1 minute. Add the onion and snow peas and stir-fry until the peas are crisp-tender, about 2 minutes. Transfer the mixture to a bowl.

Add the remaining 1 tablespoon vegetable oil to wok, then add the remaining ginger, garlic, and chiles and stir-fry until fragrant, about 1 minute. Increase the heat to high, add the chicken and stir-fry until it is cooked through, about 5 minutes.

Return the vegetables to the wok. Add the reserved sauce and bring to a simmer. Stir in about 2 teaspoons of the cornstarch-water mixture (slurry), or just enough to thicken the sauce.

Remove the ginger from the wok and stir in the peanuts. Garnish with extra red chiles for color (though you probably won't want to eat them), and serve at once.

25 minutes

Serves 4

- 8 small corn tortillas
- 1 pound fresh tomatillos (see Note, page 43)
- ½ large onion, coarsely chopped
- 1 jalapeño chile, stemmed
- ¼ bunch fresh cilantro, stemmed
- ¼ teaspoon salt

  Freshly ground pepper to taste

  Pinch of sugar
- 10 ounces boneless, skinless roast turkey
- ¼ cup low-fat sour cream

Tomatillo Turkey Tacos

Barely cooked, the chunky fresh salsa in this recipe has the acidic taste of fresh tomatillos, as well as cilantro and jalapeño chiles. This recipe is a great way to use up bits of leftover turkey from Thanksgiving, or even leftover rotisserie chicken. The recipe also makes a nice enchilada stuffing. Serve with refried beans.

Preheat the oven to 350°F.

Wrap the tortillas tightly in foil and place in the oven until heated through, about 10 minutes. Or, to use a microwave, stack the tortillas in alternating layers with damp paper towels and heat in the microwave on half power for 20 seconds. Check to see whether they are warm, and repeat if necessary. Wrap the tortillas in aluminum foil or a clean towel to keep warm and set aside.

Meanwhile, remove the papery husk from the tomatillos, then rinse and cut in half. Combine the tomatillos, onion, jalapeño, cilantro, salt, pepper, and sugar in a food processor. Process until combined but still slightly chunky.

Chop the turkey into small pieces; you should have about 2 cups. Stir together with the salsa in a saucepan and place over medium-low heat until heated through, about 5 minutes. Alternatively, mix the turkey and salsa in a microwave-safe container and heat until the turkey is warmed through, about 3 minutes, stirring once.

To serve, bring the tortillas and turkey mixture to the table and let diners help themselves, filling the tortillas with the turkey and topping their tacos with sour cream.

PER SERVING: 301 calories, 26 g protein, 33 g carbohydrate, 8 g fat (3 g saturated), 60 mg cholesterol, 209 mg sodium, 5 g fiber

Browned Sausages with Napa Cabbage Braise

I came up with this dish one night when the only vegetable in our fridge was napa cabbage. It's a play on traditional German braised cabbage, which is made with red or green cabbage and takes about an hour to cook. Napa cabbage, however, which has a long shape and frilly white-green leaves, is so tender that it can be braised in less than 10 minutes. Of course the texture and flavor aren't the same as in the original dish, but the cabbage still tastes great when combined with onions and apples for that sweet-and-savory flavor that goes so well with sausages. If you like, serve it with roasted or boiled potatoes.

Heat the olive oil in a sauté pan over medium heat. Add the sausage and brown for a few minutes on both sides. Remove from the pan with tongs, leaving the oil in the pan, and cover with foil.

Add the onion to the pan and sauté until softened, 3 minutes. Add the cabbage, stir to wilt slightly, then add the apple, garlic, wine, mustard, salt, and pepper. Add the broth, bring to a simmer, cover, and cook until the cabbage and apples are tender, 5 to 8 minutes. If the cabbage seems too juicy, simmer uncovered for a minute or two until the liquid is reduced.

If the sausages have cooled down too much, add them to the pan and simmer gently, uncovered, for a few minutes until reheated. Serve at once.

25 minutes

Serves 4

- 1 tablespoon olive oil
- 6 precooked chicken-apple sausages, cut in half lengthwise
- ½ onion, sliced
- 1 large head napa cabbage, sliced thinly crosswise
- ½ tart green apple, cored and thinly sliced
- 2 cloves garlic, chopped
- ½ cup dry red wine
- ½ teaspoon mustard
  Salt and freshly ground pepper to taste
- ½ cup low-sodium chicken broth

PER SERVING: 370 calories, 24 g protein, 12 g carbohydrate, 25 g fat (7 g saturated), 120 mg cholesterol, 977 mg sodium, 5 g fiber

40 minutes

Serves 4

1 small spaghetti squash (about 3 pounds)

Salt to taste

½ cup pine nuts

12 ounces mild Italian poultry sausage

1 tablespoon olive oil

½ onion, chopped

1 cup low-sodium chicken broth

1 14½-ounce can chopped tomatoes, drained

Freshly ground pepper to taste

Spaghetti Squash with Poultry Sausage Ragu

Available in many colors, shapes, and sizes, bumpy, striped, and polka-dotted, winter squashes look almost too pretty to eat. Their tough skins can fend off all but the sharpest of chef's knives, but once you're inside, the flesh is a beautiful shade of orange to harvest gold and tastes delicious. Spaghetti squash, a large canary-yellow gourd, takes really well to steaming, a method that results in a less intense flavor than roasting but takes about a third as long. The mild-flavored squash, which naturally separates into noodlelike strands, can be used as a substitute for pasta, tossed with a quick sausage ragu. Adding chicken broth to the sauce makes it lighter than most ragus, and the toasted pine nuts provide a lovely contrast of textures.

Cut the spaghetti squash in half lengthwise, scrape out the seeds, and cut the halves in half again. Place the squash quarters skin side down in a steamer, sprinkle with salt, and steam until tender when pierced with the tip of a small sharp knife, 15 to 20 minutes. Alternatively, place the squash quarters cut side down in a glass dish, fill with about ½ inch of water, cover, and microwave on high until tender, 10 to 12 minutes. Set aside to cool.

While the squash is cooking, toast the pine nuts in a frying pan over medium-low heat until lightly browned, about 5 minutes. Watch carefully, as they can burn easily. Remove from the pan and let cool.

Remove the sausage from its casing and cut into chunks. Heat the olive oil in a sauté pan over medium-high heat, then add the sausage and brown, 3 to 4 minutes. Remove the sausage from the pan with a slotted spoon and set aside. Add the onion and cook until tender, about 8 minutes. Add the broth and deglaze the pan, stirring to scrape up any bits that may have stuck to the bottom, then return the sausage and add the tomatoes to the pan. Bring to a simmer and cook until the sausage is thoroughly cooked, 5 minutes. Season with salt and pepper.

Use a fork to separate the flesh of the squash into strands. Toss the squash with the sausage mixture and taste again for seasoning. To serve, divide among shallow bowls and top with the pine nuts.

PER SERVING: 356 calories, 23 g protein, 19 g carbohydrate, 21 g fat (5 g saturated), 55 mg cholesterol, 856 mg sodium, 4 g fiber

Pork, Beef, and Lamb

*Facing page: Rib-eye Steak &
Portobello Mushrooms with
Tarragon Butter (recipe on page
155). Maple-Glazed Pork Chops
with Smashed Yams (recipe on
page 145)*

Because pork, beef, and lamb have so much natural flavor, they offer lots of irresistible options for quick meals. I love to splurge on the occasional juicy rib-eye steak or rack of lamb, but more often I turn to lesser cuts such as flank steak and shoulder lamb chops. Though more fibrous and chewy than the fancier cuts, they are also packed with flavor.

These less expensive meats benefit from marinating and being cooked with high, dry heat, whether that means grilling, broiling, pan-frying, or stir-frying. A thick, roasted piece of flank steak is at its best at medium-rare or medium. And after the beef has rested, it's vital to cut it very thinly across the grain.

At my house, sausage with potatoes and sauerkraut or a salad is a favorite workday dinner. I also like to play around with ground pork in various guises. A lighter choice is boneless pork loin chops, which are kind of like the pork version of boneless, skinless chicken breasts. They do well broiled or pan-fried and serve as a blank canvas for various flavors and preparations.

Red meat falls in and out of fashion with the latest health study or diet craze. There are also a lot of environmental concerns around the production of beef and pork, so eating them is not a simple choice for many people. I tend to look at preparing most kinds of meat—as well as chicken—as a special occasion, and I am willing to spend more on quality meats that come from producers who care about the animals' health and the environment, not to mention my family's well-being.

30 minutes

Serves 4

1 pound unpeeled
   red potatoes, cut
   into 1-inch pieces

   Salt to taste

4 large precooked
   bratwurst sausages

2 tablespoons vegetable
   oil

½ onion, chopped

2 tablespoons white
   wine vinegar

2 teaspoons Dijon or
   other mustard, plus
   more for serving

   Freshly ground pepper
   to taste

½ bunch chives, cut
   into 1-inch lengths

Bratwurst with Warm Potato Salad

Bratwurst is a traditional German sausage made of veal and pork that usually is sold precooked. It has a delicate flavor that makes it worth seeking out, but almost any other sausage would also go well with the potato salad. Unlike its cold and creamy cousins, this warm salad has a nice tang that offsets the rich sausages. I like serving this dish with lightly dressed sliced cucumbers.

Place the potatoes in a saucepan and add just enough water to cover by 1 inch. Season well with salt, cover, and bring to a boil. Reduce the heat to a simmer and cook, uncovered, until tender, 6 to 8 minutes.

Begin heating the sausages. You can fry them in a nonstick frying pan with a little vegetable oil, or steam them on top of the potatoes if your pot has a steamer insert.

Heat the oil in a frying pan over medium heat. Add the onion and sauté until slightly tender, about 4 minutes. Remove the pan from the heat and stir in the vinegar and mustard.

When the potatoes are done, drain them and add them to the onions. Stir to coat, then season with salt and pepper. Stir in the chives, then serve with the sausages and some mustard on the side.

PER SERVING: 413 calories,
14 g protein, 23 g carbohydrate,
29 g fat (9 g saturated),
51 mg cholesterol,
543 mg sodium, 2 g fiber

Italian Sausage with Polenta & Tomato Sauce

This comforting dish tastes as if it must have taken longer than 30 minutes to prepare. I don't think anything works as well with soft polenta as spicy Italian sausage and fresh-tasting tomato sauce. Keep the sausage in large pieces instead of crumbling it into the sauce so that it contrasts nicely with the creamy polenta. Because of the saltiness and spiciness of the sausage, you don't need to season the tomato sauce. (See photo on page 160.)

In a large sauté pan, heat ½ tablespoon of the olive oil over medium-low heat. Add the onion and sauté, stirring occasionally, until soft and slightly golden, about 10 minutes. Add the tomatoes and simmer for 10 minutes.

Meanwhile, heat the remaining ½ tablespoon olive oil in a frying pan over medium-high heat. Add the sausage and brown, 3 to 4 minutes (don't crumble the sausage—try to leave it in large chunks). Remove with a slotted spoon, then add the sausage to the tomato sauce and let it simmer until fully cooked, about 5 minutes, while you prepare the polenta.

Bring 3½ cups of water to a boil. Combine the polenta and salt in a saucepan. Add the boiling water to the polenta all at once and cook over low heat, stirring occasionally, for 5 minutes.

Serve the polenta in shallow bowls, topped with the sausage and tomato sauce.

30 minutes

Serves 4

1 tablespoon extra virgin olive oil

1 large onion, cut into large dice

1 28-ounce can unsalted chopped tomatoes

4 spicy Italian sausages (about 1 pound), removed from casings and cut into 2-inch pieces

1 cup instant polenta (see Tip)

Pinch of salt

TIP: Instant polenta is sold at Italian delis and specialty supermarkets. If you can't find it, you can make the No-Stir Polenta (see page 165) or look for prepared polenta in the refrigerated case in the supermarket. Slice into ½-inch rounds, place the rounds on a greased baking sheet, and bake on a rack about 4 inches from the heating element of a 450°F oven until crisp but creamy in the center, about 4 minutes per side.

PER SERVING: 578 calories, 29 g protein, 36 g carbohydrate, 37 g fat (14 g saturated), 101 mg cholesterol, 1,478 mg sodium, 6 g fiber

20 minutes

Serves 3 to 4

1   pound ground pork

2   tablespoons Asian fish sauce

1   teaspoon sugar

3   narrow stalks lemongrass

1½   tablespoons vegetable oil

2   shallots, minced

1 to 2   serrano chiles, thinly sliced

½   cup low-sodium chicken broth

    Leaves from 1 to 2 sprigs fresh basil, thinly sliced

Thai-Style Minced Pork with Chile & Basil

This is a simplified version of a popular Thai dish that usually contains a few more hard-to-find herbs and spices, such as opal basil, which is a purplish color and has a pronounced anise flavor. Because it's generally only available in Asian groceries, here I've substituted the Mediterranean-style basil available in every supermarket. The dish's spiciness is balanced by the salty fish sauce, the fragrant lemongrass, and a little sugar that brings out the natural sweetness of the meat. If you can't find lemongrass, try using about a tablespoon of peeled, minced fresh ginger for a different flavor. Serve over steamed jasmine or short-grain rice with Stir-Fried Greens (see page 162), if you like.

Place the pork in a bowl and, using your hands, mix in the fish sauce and sugar. Set aside to marinate.

Peel the outer layers from the lemongrass. Trim the rough end, then trim off the long narrow stalk so you're left with only the bulbous part, about 3 inches long. Thinly slice then finely chop the bulb.

Heat ½ tablespoon of the oil in a wok or large frying pan. Add the lemongrass, shallots, and chiles and sauté until lightly browned, about 5 minutes. Add the remaining 1 tablespoon oil and increase the heat to high. Add the ground pork, chopping it into small pieces with a spatula as it quickly browns. Continue stir-frying until the pork no longer has traces of pink, about another 2 minutes. Stir in the chicken broth and heat through.

Remove from the heat, stir in the basil, and serve at once.

NOTE: Many markets and butchers carry ground pork, sometimes sold frozen, so ask if you don't see it displayed. (Frozen pork must be defrosted in the refrigerator overnight.) Ground pork has so much flavor that it's great in simple recipes such as this one, but it's relatively high in fat. Ground turkey or chicken would be a leaner alternative.

PER SERVING: 369 calories, 20 g protein, 3 g carbohydrate, 29 g fat (9 g saturated), 82 mg cholesterol, 769 mg sodium, 0 g fiber

Maple-Glazed Pork Chops with Smashed Yams

Adding sweet flavors to pork helps bring out the meat's natural sweetness, but you don't want to go too far or you could end up with dessert. In this dish, which also features slightly sweet yams, maple syrup is complemented by savory chicken broth and vinegar to create a complex but easy sauce. Try serving it with sautéed spinach. (See photo on page 141.)

Preheat the broiler, placing the rack about 4 inches from the heating element, and line a baking sheet with aluminum foil.

Place the sweet potatoes in a saucepan and add enough water to cover. Season with salt. Bring to a boil, reduce to a simmer, and cook until tender, 10 to 15 minutes. Drain the potatoes and set aside.

While the potatoes are cooking, rub both sides of the pork chops with salt and pepper. Stir the maple syrup, chicken broth, vinegar, and mustard together in a small saucepan.

Brush the chops with some of this mixture and reserve the rest for the sauce. Place the chops on the prepared baking sheet and broil until cooked through, about 4 minutes per side. Tent with foil while you finish the dish.

Bring the reserved sauce to a simmer in a small saucepan over low heat. Stir the cornstarch mixture (slurry) into the sauce and simmer until it thickens. After the meat has rested, pour the collected juices into the sauce.

Mash the sweet potatoes coarsely with the butter and season with salt and pepper. Prop the chops against a mound of the potatoes on serving plates, drizzle with the sauce, and serve.

> **NOTE:** If you purchase smaller center-cut chops, which are sometimes only 4 ounces each, you may want to serve two chops per person. If the chops are thicker than 1 inch, you will also need to increase the cooking time by a minute or two per side.

25 minutes

Serves 4

- 2 pounds garnet sweet potatoes, peeled and cut into eighths
- 4 boneless center-cut pork chops, about 6 ounces each
- Salt and freshly ground pepper to taste
- 2 tablespoons maple syrup
- 2 tablespoons chicken broth or water
- ½ cup apple cider vinegar
- ½ teaspoon whole-grain mustard
- ½ teaspoon cornstarch mixed with 1 tablespoon water
- 2 to 3 tablespoons unsalted butter

PER SERVING: 567 calories, 44 g protein, 63 g carbohydrate, 15 g fat (7 g saturated), 133 mg cholesterol, 130 mg sodium, 6 g fiber

20 minutes

Serves 3 to 4

1 10-ounce package
   of refrigerated
   pizza dough

1 14½-ounce can
   chopped tomatoes,
   drained

   Salt and freshly
   ground pepper
   to taste

½ teaspoon
   dried oregano

1 tablespoon extra
   virgin olive oil, plus
   more for drizzling

½ ounce chunk
   Parmesan cheese

1 teaspoon fresh
   lemon juice

4 cups baby arugula
   leaves or coarsely
   chopped mature
   arugula

6 slices prosciutto

Pizza with Arugula & Prosciutto

If you spread out refrigerated pizza dough as thinly as possible and bake it in a very hot oven, it bakes up to a crisp-thin crust. Be sure the oven is completely preheated before cooking. Adding fresh arugula immediately before serving turns the dish into a salad and a pizza in one.

Preheat the oven to 500°F. Grease an 11- by 16-inch baking sheet with olive oil.

Unroll the pizza dough on top of the prepared baking sheet. With your fingers, spread the dough thinly and evenly almost to the edges of the pan. Spread the tomatoes very thinly over the dough, leaving a 1-inch border around the edges. Sprinkle with salt, pepper, and oregano. Drizzle the entire pizza, including the edges, with olive oil.

When the oven is completely preheated, bake the pizza until the edges of the crust are golden and the middle is completely cooked, 8 to 10 minutes.

Meanwhile, using a sharp vegetable peeler, shave the Parmesan into thin strips; set aside.

Whisk together the 1 tablespoon olive oil and the lemon juice and season with salt and pepper. Toss the arugula in enough of this dressing to lightly moisten it, taste, and add more salt and pepper, if necessary.

Remove the pizza from the oven. Cover it immediately with a layer of prosciutto slices. Top with the dressed arugula and the Parmesan shavings and serve.

PER SERVING: 320 calories, 20 g protein, 35 g carbohydrate, 11 g fat (3 g saturated), 25 mg cholesterol, 1,585 mg sodium, 2 g fiber

TIP: If you're serving the pizza to children, omit the arugula and substitute leftover cooked shredded chicken for the prosciutto; just add it on top of the tomatoes so that it cooks with the pizza. This would also be a good choice for people on a low-sodium diet, since prosciutto is high in salt.

20 minutes

Serves 4

8   ounces wide egg
     noodles

1½ tablespoons
     unsalted butter

4   boneless center-cut
     pork chops, about
     6 ounces each

    Salt and freshly
    ground pepper
    to taste

¼   cup brandy

2   tablespoons
     orange juice

1   tablespoon bitter
     orange marmalade

Orange-Glazed Pork Chops with Buttered Noodles

Pork chops taste best when they're not too well-done, even though many of us have grown used to eating them somewhat dried out. As the noodles cook, you can quickly pan-fry the pork chops, then deglaze the pan with a shot of brandy. Orange marmalade and butter complete the sauce.

Bring a large pot of salted water to a boil, then cook the noodles according to the package directions. After draining them, stir in ½ tablespoon of the butter. Season with salt and pepper and keep warm.

While the noodles are cooking, season the pork chops on both sides with salt and pepper.

Over medium-high heat, melt ½ tablespoon of the butter in a nonstick frying pan large enough to fit all 4 chops snugly. Add the chops to the pan and cook until browned and mostly cooked through, about 4 minutes per side. Transfer the chops to a plate and tent with foil.

Take the pan off the heat for a few moments to allow it to cool slightly. Add a spoonful of brandy; if it evaporates immediately, the pan is still too hot; allow it to cool a few moments more. Return the pan to medium heat and add the rest of the brandy. Cook until the brandy is reduced by half. Stir in the orange juice and the marmalade until it melts. The glaze should have a thick, jamlike consistency at this point. Stir in the remaining ½ tablespoon butter until melted. Season with salt and pepper.

Return the chops and their accumulated juices to the pan and cook, turning once, until they are heated through and coated with the glaze. Serve the chops on the noodles, drizzled with the remaining glaze.

[**NOTE:** The bitter orange of the marmalade and the sweetness of the pork are complemented well by brandy. Substituting Cognac is a special treat, and even bourbon is a nice substitution.]

PER SERVING: 516 calories, 46 g protein, 38 g carbohydrate, 15 g fat (6 g saturated), 175 mg cholesterol, 85 mg sodium, 2 g fiber

Beef Stroganoff

Many Americans remember beef stroganoff—tender sliced beef, onions, and mushrooms tied together with a creamy sauce—from their childhood. I like to serve it over noodles, but you might prefer to eat it with rice or potatoes. This version is lighter than most, because the sauce isn't thickened with flour; instead, it's made with a small amount of broth and low-fat sour cream. Buying presliced mushrooms and using shallots rather than the more traditional onions speed up the cooking process.

Bring a large pot of salted water to a boil.

Meanwhile, toss the beef slices with plenty of salt and pepper to taste.

Heat a large frying pan over medium-high heat. When it is very hot, add the oil. When the oil shimmers, add about one-third of the meat, spreading it out so that it's flat in the pan; avoid crowding the pan. Brown for no more than 1 minute per side, then transfer to a shallow dish. Repeat with the remaining beef slices.

Reduce the heat to medium. Add the brandy and deglaze the pan, stirring to scrape up any bits that may have stuck to the bottom, and simmer until reduced, about 1 minute. Pour the contents of the pan over the meat.

At this point, start cooking the noodles according to the package directions. When the noodles are done, drain, allowing a little water to cling to the noodles. Return the noodles to the pot and toss with ½ to 1 tablespoon of the butter. Keep warm.

Melt another tablespoon of the butter in the pan over medium heat, then add the shallots. Stir until just softened, then add the mushrooms. Allow to brown and soften for a few minutes. Add the broth, return to a steady simmer, and cook until the broth reduces by half, about 5 minutes. Add the meat and juices to the pan, simmer for 1 minute (there won't be a lot of liquid), remove from the heat, and stir in the sour cream until incorporated. Season the sauce with pepper to taste and add salt, if needed. If the sauce is too thick, add a little more broth and heat gently.

Serve the stroganoff over the noodles with plenty of sauce, garnished with the parsley.

TIP: After you brown the meat, remove it from the pan, then briefly return it to the sauce to combine. It should not linger there, however, or it will become tough.

---

35 minutes

Serves 4

- 1 pound beef sirloin or New York steak, fat removed, meat sliced very thinly against the grain into 1- by 2-inch pieces
- Salt and freshly ground pepper to taste
- 2 teaspoons vegetable oil
- 2 tablespoons brandy
- 8 ounces egg noodles or other flat, short noodles, such as farfalle
- 1½ to 2 tablespoons butter
- ½ cup sliced shallots
- 8 ounces presliced mushrooms
- 1 cup low-sodium beef broth, plus more if needed
- ½ cup low-fat sour cream
- Chopped fresh Italian (flat-leaf) parsley for garnish

PER SERVING: 510 calories, 38 g protein, 43 g carbohydrate, 19 g fat (8 g saturated), 144 mg cholesterol, 372 mg sodium, 2 g fiber

20 minutes

Serves 4

1 pound flank steak

Salt and freshly
ground pepper
to taste

2 teaspoons
vegetable oil

3 cloves garlic,
thinly sliced

20 ounces pre-washed
spinach

¼ cup oyster sauce

Sesame seeds
for garnish

Beef & Spinach Stir-Fry with Oyster Sauce

Simple dishes flavored with oyster sauce are common in Cantonese cooking, which relies on the quality of fresh ingredients rather than intensely flavored spices. In this recipe, the spinach is cooked separately so that the liquid it releases does not make the meat chewy. In the end, the two are brought together with sizzling garlic and oyster sauce. This recipe will be done in the time it takes to steam some short- or medium-grain rice.

Place the flank steak flat on a work surface and cut it along the grain into two or three long, 3-inch-wide sections. Working with one section, cut it with a very sharp knife, this time against the grain, as thinly as you can, about ⅛ inch thick. Repeat with the remaining sections of steak. Season the meat slices with salt and a generous amount of pepper; set aside.

Place a wok or nonstick frying pan over medium-high heat. When hot, add 1 teaspoon of the oil and heat until sizzling. Add half of the garlic and cook until slightly browned. Add a few handsful of spinach to the wok and stir. As the spinach wilts, keep adding more, stirring constantly until it has all wilted.

Remove the spinach from the pan and place in a colander set over a bowl. Set aside to allow the liquid to drain out. Pour off and discard any liquid remaining in the wok.

Increase the heat to high and add the remaining teaspoon of oil to the wok. When it is hot, add the remaining garlic and cook, stirring, until slightly browned. Add the flank steak and sauté quickly, stirring often, until the meat is just browned, about 2 minutes.

Press the spinach to remove any remaining water, then return it to the pan. Stir in the oyster sauce, season with pepper, and heat through. Serve garnished with sesame seeds.

NOTE: Oyster sauce, a thick, savory sauce flavored with oyster extracts, is available in the Asian foods section of most supermarkets.

PER SERVING: 265 calories,
28 g protein, 12 g carbohydrate,
12 g fat (4 g saturated),
59 mg cholesterol,
1,085 mg sodium, 4 fiber

Black Pepper Beef
with Cucumber Salad

30 minutes

Serves 4

Salting the cucumbers in this recipe helps the dressing cling to the salad better and gives the cucumbers a crisp, cool texture that contrasts well with the savory beef. If you can find black sesame seeds, they add a nice contrast in color, but regular sesame seeds are fine, too. The same goes for the fresh red chile peppers, which add some color, if you can find them. Serve with steamed short- or medium-grain rice.

Crush the peppercorns with a heavy skillet or with a mortar and pestle. Combine the soy sauce, oyster sauce, and peppercorns in a shallow baking dish. Place the meat in the mixture, turning to coat both sides. Set aside to marinate.

Meanwhile, peel the cucumbers and cut in half lengthwise. Cut the cucumbers into thin half moons, then place in a bowl and sprinkle with 1 teaspoon salt. Toss to combine and set aside.

Heat a large frying pan over high heat. When it's very hot, add the oil. When the oil is shimmering but not yet smoking, remove the meat from the marinade and place it in the pan. Cook until medium-rare, 5 to 7 minutes per side. Transfer to a plate and tent with foil; set aside.

Combine the ginger, jalapeño, vinegar, and sesame oil. Put the cucumbers in a colander and rinse well, then shake to rid of the excess water. Pat dry with paper towels. Combine the cucumbers and the vinegar-oil mixture in a serving bowl and toss to combine. Top with the optional sesame seeds.

Slice the meat against the grain and divide it among serving plates. Pass the cucumber salad at the table.

> **NOTE:** English hothouse cucumbers (usually sold wrapped in plastic) have a better flavor than waxed cucumbers, and they don't need to be seeded. If you use waxed cucumbers, scrape the seeds out with a small spoon after you halve the cucumbers.

2	teaspoons black peppercorns
½	cup soy sauce
2	tablespoons oyster sauce (see Note, page 150)
1½	pounds flank steak
2	English hothouse cucumbers
1	teaspoon salt
1 to 2	tablespoons vegetable oil
1	1-inch piece fresh ginger, peeled and finely minced or grated (see Tip, page 30)
1	red or green jalapeño or other fresh red chile, seeded and minced (see Tip, page 26)
3	tablespoons unseasoned rice vinegar
½	teaspoon Asian sesame oil
1	teaspoon black or white sesame seeds

PER SERVING: 600 calories, 40 g protein, 59 g carbohydrate, 22 g fat (8 g saturated), 84 mg cholesterol, 136 mg sodium, 4 g fiber. The calories and other nutrients absorbed from marinades vary and are difficult to estimate, so the marinade is not included in this analysis.

30 minutes

Serves 6

- 2 pounds flank steak
- 3 cloves garlic, minced
  Salt and freshly ground pepper to taste
- 1½ tablespoons olive oil
- 1 bunch thin asparagus, trimmed

CHIMICHURRI

- 1 clove garlic, minced
- ½ cup minced sweet onion
- ½ cup minced fresh Italian (flat-leaf) parsley
- 1½ teaspoons salt
  Freshly ground pepper to taste
- ¼ cup red wine vinegar
- ½ cup olive oil

Flank Steak
with Chimichurri & Asparagus

Chimichurri, a delicious sauce from Argentina made from olive oil, herbs, and onions, is usually paired with grilled meat. Asparagus is a natural partner for both. When you add it to the grill or broiler, it gets a little crunchy and golden on the outside and creamy inside. Thinner asparagus does better at such high heat. Serve with rice or bread.

If you plan to use a grill, prepare a fire or preheat a gas grill for cooking over medium-high heat. Or, preheat the broiler, placing one rack about 4 inches from the heating element and the other rack several inches away.

Rub the steak with two-thirds of the garlic and season liberally on both sides with salt and pepper. Coat with about ½ tablespoon olive oil.

Toss the asparagus with the remaining garlic and the remaining 1 tablespoon olive oil. Season with salt and pepper.

If you are using a grill, grill the steak for 5 to 6 minutes, turn, and grill until medium-rare, 5 to 6 minutes more. When the steak is done, remove it from the grill, tent with foil, and let rest for at least 5 minutes. Put the asparagus on the grill and cook, turning often, until crisp-tender, 2 to 3 minutes for thin spears and about 10 minutes for very thick spears.

If you are using a broiler, place the steak and the asparagus on separate baking sheets lined with aluminum foil. Place the steak directly under the broiler and the asparagus on a lower rack. Broil for 5 to 6 minutes. Turn the steak and asparagus once and continue broiling until medium-rare, 5 to 6 minutes more. Remove the steak from the broiler, tent with foil, and let rest for 5 minutes. If the asparagus is not yet done, reduce the heat to 450°F and continue cooking until crisp-tender.

To make the chimichurri, combine all the ingredients in a serving bowl and stir until the salt dissolves. Taste and add more salt, if you like.

To serve, slice the meat very thinly against the grain. Serve with the chimichurri and the asparagus.

PER SERVING: 471 calories, 34 g protein, 7 g carbohydrate, 34 g fat (8 g saturated), 78 mg cholesterol, 1,167 mg sodium, 2 g fiber

25 minutes

Serves 4

- 4 minute steaks, about 4 ounces each
- Salt to taste
- 2 teaspoons black peppercorns
- 1 tablespoon vegetable oil
- ¼ cup minced shallots
- 1 cup zinfandel or other dry red wine
- ¼ cup heavy whipping cream
- 4 tablespoons unsalted butter, cut into pieces

Minute Steak with Zinfandel–Black Pepper Sauce

Making a simple pan sauce with wine is one of the easiest ways to impart flavor to a steak. Zinfandel, with its characteristic peppery notes, is a perfect match for the crushed black peppercorns that coat the steaks here. Like most wines, zinfandel becomes very acidic when reduced and needs to be mellowed out with cream or butter, making this dish something of a decadent treat. When you achieve the right balance, the wine provides just enough acidity to cut through the richness of the meat. Serve with Mashed Yukon Golds (recipe on page 116).

Season the steaks on both sides with salt.

Crush the peppercorns with a heavy skillet or with a mortar and pestle. Press an equal amount into one side of each steak.

Heat a frying pan over medium-high heat until it is quite hot. Add the oil and heat until it is almost smoking. Sear each steak, pepper side down, for 1 minute. Flip over and cook another 30 seconds. Remove from the pan and place, pepper side up, on a warm platter. Tent with foil to keep warm.

In the same pan over medium heat, sauté the shallots until tender, about 2 minutes. Increase the heat to medium-high, add the wine, and deglaze the pan, stirring to scrape up any bits that may have stuck to the bottom. Cook until the liquid is reduced to about ¼ cup, 4 to 5 minutes. Reduce heat to medium-low, stir in the cream, and heat through. Remove the sauce from the heat and whisk in the butter pieces until melted.

Season the sauce with salt and serve over the steaks.

NOTE: Economical minute steaks, also known as sandwich or breakfast steaks, are about ¼ inch thick. If you opt for a fancier cut like New York strip, allow several minutes longer per side to cook or finish in a 400°F oven.

PER SERVING: 530 calories, 44 g protein, 4 g carbohydrate, 33 g fat (15 g saturated), 176 mg cholesterol, 203 mg sodium, 0 g fiber

TIP: If you omit the black peppercorns and substitute a dry white wine, you can use the same sauce with sautéed or pan-roasted chicken, pork, or fish.

Rib-Eye Steak & Portobello Mushrooms with Tarragon Butter

A pat of herb-infused butter is a wonderful addition to a hot, crusty steak, imparting its flavor to the meat as it melts. Experiment with other types of herbs—thyme, oregano, marjoram—or even spicy flavors like crushed black pepper and minced chipotle peppers. This dish is great served with microwave-baked potatoes or crusty bread. (See photo on page 140.)

Preheat the broiler, placing the rack about 4 inches from the heating element. Line a baking sheet with aluminum foil.

In a bowl, beat together the tarragon, ½ teaspoon of the rosemary, the lemon juice, salt, and butter. Place the mixture on a sheet of plastic wrap and roll into a log, wrapping tightly. Place in the freezer to chill.

Season the steaks with a liberal amount of salt and pepper; rub in the remaining 1½ teaspoons rosemary and 1 teaspoon of the olive oil.

Place the mushrooms in a bowl. Drizzle with the remaining 2 teaspoons olive oil and the vinegar and sprinkle with salt and pepper.

Place the steaks and the mushrooms, stem side up, on the prepared baking sheet. Broil for 5 to 6 minutes. Turn the steaks and broil until medium-rare, 5 to 6 minutes more. Place a slice of the chilled tarragon butter on each steak, and serve each with a mushroom.

30 minutes

Serves 4

- 2 teaspoons minced fresh tarragon
- 2 teaspoons minced fresh rosemary
- ½ teaspoon fresh lemon juice
  Salt to taste
- 4 tablespoons softened unsalted butter
- 4 boneless rib-eye steaks, 10 to 12 ounces each
  Freshly ground pepper to taste
- 3 teaspoons olive oil
- 4 large portobello mushrooms, cleaned and stemmed
- 1 teaspoon balsamic vinegar

TIP: This recipe makes twice as much tarragon butter as you will need. Store the rest in the freezer and use on vegetables or other grilled or roasted meats.

PER SERVING: 497 calories, 52 g protein, 7 g carbohydrate, 29 g fat (13 g saturated), 150 mg cholesterol, 191 mg sodium, 5 g fiber

25 minutes

Serves 4

- 3 tablespoons extra virgin olive oil, plus more for brushing
- 4 cloves garlic, minced
- 2 15-ounce cans chickpeas, drained and rinsed
- ¾ cup low-sodium chicken broth

  Salt and freshly ground pepper to taste
- 6 tablespoons balsamic, raspberry, or other fruity vinegar

  Leaves from 2 sprigs fresh mint, minced
- 4 round-bone shoulder lamb chops, ½ to ¾ inch thick each

  Mixed baby salad greens, watercress, or arugula

Grilled Lamb Shoulder Chops with Chickpeas

This is a great dish for last-minute entertaining. If you have chickpeas and a fruity vinegar in your pantry, the only thing you need to pick up at the store is lamb chops and fresh mint. Cooking the lamb chops is easy, too; simply throw them in a grill pan, then deglaze the pan with the vinegar. When you drizzle the fruity sauce on the rich, caramelized meat, it will taste just as if it had been marinating for hours, and the greens will soak up all the flavorful juices.

Heat the 3 tablespoons olive oil in a large sauté pan and sauté the garlic until fragrant, about 1 minute. Add the chickpeas and ½ cup of the broth and season with salt and pepper. Simmer, stirring often, for 5 minutes. Stir in 2 tablespoons of the vinegar and the mint, taste, adjust the amount of salt and pepper, and remove from the heat.

Meanwhile, trim the fat from the chops and make one cut through each chop near the bone so that they don't curl up during cooking. Season the lamb chops on both sides with salt and pepper and brush with olive oil.

Heat a seasoned grill pan over medium-high heat. Grill the lamb chops until medium-rare, about 3 to 4 minutes per side. Remove the chops from the pan, tent with foil, and let rest.

Combine the remaining ¼ cup vinegar and the remaining ¼ cup broth, then add it to hot grill pan and deglaze, stirring to scrape up any bits that may have stuck to the bottom. Cook for 2 minutes, allowing the liquid to reduce.

Divide the baby greens among serving plates, top with the lamb chops and chickpeas, and drizzle both with the pan sauce. Serve, passing more of the sauce at the table.

[**NOTE:** Round-bone shoulder chops aren't as tender as rib chops, but they have lots of flavor and are less expensive.]

PER SERVING: 393 calories, 27 g protein, 25 g carbohydrate, 20 g fat (5 g saturated), 69 mg cholesterol, 403 mg sodium, 8 g fiber

TIP: Some canned chickpeas are less salty than others. Be sure to season the beans well to bring out their garlicky flavor.

40 minutes

Serves 4

12 ounces green beans, trimmed and snapped in half if large

1¼ teaspoons ground cumin

¾ teaspoon salt, plus more to taste

¾ teaspoon freshly ground pepper, plus more to taste

8 small double-rib lamb chops, about 2 pounds total

1 cup instant couscous

3 tablespoons finely chopped shallots

1 teaspoon coarsely chopped fresh mint, Italian (flat-leaf) parsley, or basil

3 tablespoons sherry vinegar or red wine vinegar

1½ tablespoons extra virgin olive oil

Cumin Lamb Chops with Couscous & Green Bean Salad

In this recipe, lamb is coated with a simple rub of cumin, salt, and pepper, making it a natural match for instant couscous, which takes only a few minutes to prepare. The accompanying green bean salad is cold and tart, the better to offset the rich meat. If you like, throw some chopped tomatoes or halved cherry tomatoes into the green bean salad.

Preheat the broiler, placing the rack about 4 inches from the heating element, and prepare a steamer for the beans. Line a baking sheet with aluminum foil.

Prepare a large bowl of ice water. Steam the beans until tender, 5 to 8 minutes. Immediately plunge the beans into the ice water. When cool, drain and pat dry.

Combine the cumin, ¾ teaspoon salt, and ¾ teaspoon pepper in a small bowl. Rub this spice mix into both sides of the lamb chops.

Place the chops on the prepared baking sheet and broil for 2 to 3 minutes per side for medium-rare, 4 to 5 minutes per side for medium. Tent with foil and let rest.

Bring the required amount of water to a boil for the couscous then prepare according to the package directions.

Meanwhile, combine the shallots, mint, vinegar, and oil in a medium bowl. Season with salt and pepper. Toss the green beans with the dressing, taste, and adjust the amount of salt and pepper, if necessary.

Serve the lamb chops on top of a bed of couscous, with the green bean salad on the side.

[**NOTE:** You can serve 2 double-rib chops per person or single-rib chops if they are large.]

PER SERVING: 424 calories, 33 g protein, 43 g carbohydrate, 13 g fat (4 g saturated), 81 mg cholesterol, 528 mg sodium, 5 g fiber

Lamb Kebabs with Creamy Hummus

Ground lamb kebabs seasoned with mint, garlic, and lemon share space on skewers with chunks of onion, bell pepper, and cherry tomatoes and then are quickly broiled or grilled. Serve them with pita and a simple creamy hummus sauce for a Mediterranean-style meal.

Preheat the broiler. Line a baking sheet with aluminum foil.

Combine the lamb with the garlic, lemon juice, salt, pepper, cinnamon, and cayenne. Place the mixture in the refrigerator briefly while you cut the onion and bell pepper into 2-inch pieces.

Form the meat mixture into 20 ovals about 2 inches long and thread each skewer with 2 ovals, 2 cherry tomatoes, and a few pieces of onion and red pepper, alternating the vegetables decoratively.

Place the kebabs on the prepared baking sheet and broil for 5 minutes. Turn over (make sure the meat is flipped) and broil until the meat is cooked through, 4 to 5 minutes more.

While the kebabs are cooking, combine the yogurt and hummus in a bowl. Season to taste with salt and pepper, if needed.

Heat the pita in the hot oven for a minute or two right before serving. Serve the kebabs with the pita and the creamy hummus.

[**NOTE:** You will need to pre-soak 10 wooden skewers in water for at least 30 minutes so they don't burn under the broiler.]

Serves 4
30 minutes

1¼	pounds lean ground lamb
4	cloves garlic, minced
2	tablespoons fresh lemon juice (from about 1 lemon)
½	teaspoon salt
	Freshly ground black pepper to taste
⅛	teaspoon ground cinnamon
¼	teaspoon cayenne pepper
½	red onion
1	red bell pepper
½	pint cherry tomatoes
½	cup nonfat plain yogurt
½	cup prepared hummus
4	large pieces pita bread, halved

PER SERVING: 541 calories, 34 g protein, 49 g carbohydrate, 23 g fat (9 g saturated), 94 mg cholesterol, 1,074 mg sodium, 5 g fiber

Side Dishes

Sometimes you might crave an extra dish of greens or a side of polenta to complement the main courses in this book. This chapter includes a few ideas for vegetable and starch side dishes that I often turn to at home. In addition, think about mixing and matching some of the easy side dishes included in the previous recipes, such as adding a pile of Sweet Potato Fries (see page 122) to the Flank Steak with Chimichurri & Asparagus (page 152).

Facing page: No-Stir Polenta (recipe on page 165), served with Italian Sausage & Tomato Sauce (recipe on page 143); Stir-Fried Greens (recipe on page 162)

15 to 20 minutes

Serves 4

1 to 2 tablespoons vegetable oil

1 to 2 cloves garlic, thinly sliced

1-inch piece ginger, sliced into 3 coins (optional)

Pinch of red pepper flakes

8 to 10 ounces stir-fry greens

Salt to taste

Stir-Fried Greens

Specialty, health food, and farmers' markets often carry what are called stir-fry or braising greens next to the bulk salad greens. They're a combination of various kinds of chard, mâche, kale, spinach, and other sturdy greens. (Don't substitute bulk salad greens, which are too delicate for cooking.) In addition, many supermarkets carry prepackaged chopped, cleaned greens like mustard greens and kale in the produce section. Or, just wash, trim, and coarsely chop a couple of bunches of kale or chard, discarding the stems. This dish goes nicely with Asian stir-fries and noodles. Or, omit the ginger, use extra virgin olive oil instead of vegetable oil, and add a squeeze of lemon juice at the end for an Italian-style side dish. (See photo on page 161.)

Heat the vegetable oil in a wok over medium-high heat, then add the garlic, ginger, and red pepper flakes. Swirl around until fragrant, then add about one-third of the greens. Stir-fry to wilt slightly, and continue adding greens until they're all slightly wilted. Add 2 tablespoons of water and a sprinkle of salt, cover, and cook until the sturdier greens are tender through the stem, 7 to 10 minutes.

Remove the ginger coins, taste, adjust the amount of salt, and serve.

PER SERVING: 49 calories, 1 g protein, 4 g carbohydrate, 4 g fat (0 g saturated), 0 mg cholesterol, 11 mg sodium, 2 fiber

Braised Endive

Though you normally see Belgian endives raw in salads or hors d'oeuvres, their deep, rustic flavor comes out best when they are braised. If you quarter them and cover them in broth and a little butter, they take about 10 minutes to simmer to tenderness. The sauce is creamy and luscious, with a bit of sugar to smooth out the vegetable's bitterness. Serve with pan-roasted chicken or fish dishes.

Trim the endive stems, then quarter through the core. Place in a stockpot wide enough so that they almost all fit in one layer, and cover with the broth, butter, sugar, salt. and pepper. Bring to a simmer, cover, and cook until very tender through the core, about 10 minutes. Taste, adjust the amount of salt and pepper, and serve.

15 minutes

Serves 4

2	pounds Belgian endives (see Note, page 98)
1½	cups low-sodium chicken broth
2	tablespoons unsalted butter, cut into pieces
½	teaspoon sugar
	Salt and freshly ground pepper to taste

PER SERVING: 107 calories, 5 g protein, 10 g carbohydrate, 6 g fat (4 g saturated), 16 mg cholesterol, 81 mg sodium, 8 g fiber

15 minutes

Serves 6

1 large globe eggplant
(about 1½ pounds)

1 clove garlic

⅓ cup tahini
(see Note, page 90)

¼ cup fresh lemon juice
(from about 2 lemons)

¼ cup extra virgin
olive oil, plus more
for drizzling

Salt to taste

¼ cup whole-milk plain
yogurt, if needed

Microwave Baba Ghanoush

Usually, making the creamy Mediterranean dip baba ghanoush requires roasting an eggplant for about 30 to 40 minutes, but in this version the eggplant cooks in about 10 minutes in the microwave. Serve at room temperature with toasted pita wedges as an appetizer or part of a meze spread with Tabbouleh and Falafel (see pages 88 and 90).

Pierce the eggplant with a small knife in a few places. Place on a microwave-safe plate, cover with plastic wrap, and microwave at high power for 4 minutes. Turn the eggplant over and microwave for 4 minutes more. If the eggplant is not yet very soft all over, cook for another minute or two per side.

Puree the garlic in a food processor.

Scrape out the softened flesh of the eggplant with a spoon. If you see any large pockets of seeds, remove them, as they can be bitter. Add the eggplant to the food processor, along with the tahini, lemon juice, and olive oil. Puree until completely combined. Season with salt and pulse a few more times.

If you like a creamier baba ghanoush, add the yogurt. Transfer to a bowl and drizzle with olive oil before serving at room temperature.

PER SERVING: 200 calories,
4 g protein, 9 g carbohydrate,
18 g fat (3 g saturated),
1 mg cholesterol, 11 mg sodium,
3 g fiber

No-Stir Polenta

Though it takes a little while to roast, this version of polenta doesn't require you to stand over a hot stove stirring for half an hour like the traditional kind. The polenta still comes out creamy and makes a nice side dish to chicken dishes or vegetarian stews. You can also use it in Italian Sausage with Polenta & Tomato Sauce (see page 143). Just start it a half hour in advance of quick-cooking recipes. (See photo on page 160.)

Preheat the oven to 350°F.

Butter a 13- by 9-inch pan. Combine the polenta and salt with 7 cups warm water in the pan, dot with butter, and roast, uncovered, for 50 minutes. Stir the top grains with a fork, then continue cooking until the grains are no longer crunchy, 10 minutes more. Serve warm.

1 hour, 5 minutes
(active time 10 minutes)

Serves 10

2   cups polenta

2   teaspoons salt

3   tablespoons unsalted butter

PER SERVING: 289 calories, 6 g protein, 47 g carbohydrate, 8 g fat (4 g saturated), 19 mg cholesterol, 932 mg sodium, 2 g fiber

Glossary

Below you will find some techniques and ingredients included in the book. The ingredients are available at ethnic and specialty markets, and supermarkets with large ethnic or gourmet sections.

Achiote paste A Mexican seasoning made of ground annatto seeds, spices, vinegar, and sometimes garlic. Sold in blocks.

Anaheim chiles Long and narrow fresh chiles that are the color of green bell peppers. They are slightly spicy but fruity.

Asian fish sauce An intensely flavored (and intensely aromatic) sauce made of salted, fermented anchovies or other fish that is essential to Southeast Asian cooking.

Basmati rice A fragrant long-grain rice used in Indian and Middle Eastern cooking.

Bok choy A juicy and crunchy member of the Chinese cabbage family with a delicate flavor. The large white and green bok choy and the smaller light-green baby bok choy are usually interchangeable, though the larger one takes longer to cook.

Chickpeas Also known as garbanzo beans, these beige, round legumes have a nutty flavor and dense, snappy texture, even when canned.

Clockwise from left: Japanese rice wine (Mirin),oyster sauce, chipotle chiles, saffron (above chiles),Chinese black beans, lemongrass, shallot, shiitake mushrooms, pepitas, serrano chiles, poblano chile, and rice stick noodles.

Chiffonade To cut delicate herbs, such as basil and mint leaves, into very thin ribbons. Stack the leaves, gently roll them up, then thinly slice across the roll.

Chipotle chiles Dried and smoked jalapeño chiles, often sold canned en adobo, which means marinated in a deliciously smoky, very spicy sauce.

Coconut milk An important ingredient in Southeast Asian cooking, coconut milk is actually coconut milk steeped in hot water, then drained. It is available in "lite" versions that work fine for the recipes in this book. The cream usually rises to the top, so shake the can before opening.

Couscous A tiny-grained wheat pasta from North Africa.

Dice To chop food into uniform cubes. Fine dice are smaller than ¼ inch, small dice are ¼ inch, medium dice are slightly less than ½ inch, and large dice are around ¾ inch.

Fontina cheese A semifirm Italian cheese with a creamy, mild flavor. Substitute with mozzarella or Monterey jack.

Jalapeño chiles Small dark green or red fresh chile peppers that are usually 2 to 3 inches long and squat, with a pointed tip. Their considerable heat is greatly reduced if you remove the seeds and membrane.

Jicama A juicy, crunchy root vegetable popular in Latin America. It has a brown, papery skin that must be peeled.

Julienne To cut food into thin strips, usually ⅛ by ⅛ by 1 to 2 inches.

Lemongrass An aromatic vegetable with a lemony scent used in Southeast Asian cooking. When shopping for it, look for stalks that have plump, bulbous ends, the part usually used in cooking.

Lentils My favorite are French green lentils, or lentilles du Puy, which stay firmer when cooked than the larger regular green lentils.

Mince To chop very finely.

Olive oil Extra virgin olive oil is made from the first cold pressing of olives. Regular olive oil is of lesser quality because it usually contains oil that is extracted with the help of chemicals. However, quality varies greatly among extra virgin olive oils. It's good to have on hand a large bottle of less expensive extra virgin or regular olive oil for cooking, plus a better-quality one for Italian and Mediterranean dishes that call for a swirl of olive oil at the end.

Orzo A small rice-shaped Italian pasta.

Oyster sauce A thick, savory Chinese sauce flavored with oyster extracts. Some sauces have more oyster flavor than others.

Panko High-quality dried bread crumbs from Japan. If they're not available, substitute unseasoned dry bread crumbs.

Parmesan cheese A hard cow's milk cheese from Italy. Authentic imported Parmesan cheese, labeled Parmigiano-Reggiano, is worth the investment if you love pasta. It has a deeper flavor and finer texture than domestic versions. Italy's grana padano is a good choice, too.

Pecorino cheese Aged pecorino is a hard Italian sheep's milk cheese that is often grated over pasta. It has a more acidic flavor than Parmesan.

Pepitas Shelled green pumpkin seeds. When toasted, they make a crunchy snack or salad topping.

Poblano chile Sometimes labeled pasilla, this fresh chile is blackish green and about the size of a green bell pepper, with a more tapered shape.

Portobello An oversize button mushroom with a dense texture. Great for grilling or roasting.

Prosciutto Cured and smoked, but not cooked, Italian ham. Imported prosciutto tends to have a better flavor and be less salty than domestic varieties. If possible, buy it freshly sliced. Presliced versions tend to be very salty.

Queso fresco A highly perishable fresh Mexican cheese with a mild, salty taste and a crumbly texture.

Rice Rice is classified by the length of its grain. Short- or medium-grain rice is used in Japanese and Chinese cooking and results in a stickier bowl of rice that's easier to eat with chopsticks. With long-grain rice, which is used in Mediterranean, Indian, and Mexican cooking, the grains stay separated after cooking.

Rice stick noodles Very thin dried rice noodles from Southeast Asia that can be soaked in hot water or cooked briefly in boiling water.

Rice vinegar This Asian vinegar has less acidity and a milder flavor than Western counterparts. It's used in several Asian cuisines for salads, sushi rice, marinades, and stir-fries. Look for bottles labeled "unseasoned" or "natural."

Rice wine Made of fermented rice, this wine is used in Chinese and Japanese cooking. Japanese varieties include both mirin and sake. Chinese rice wine is often compared to dry sherry.

Saffron Consisting of the dried, hand-picked stigmas of crocus flowers, saffron adds a heady flavor and orange-red hue to Mediterranean and Indian dishes.

Salt The recipes in this book call for table salt for simplicity's sake. I prefer to cook with kosher salt, however, because it has a cleaner flavor and dissolves more quickly. If you use kosher salt, you will need up to twice as much as table salt because of its coarser texture. Sea salt also varies in potency depending on how coarsely it is ground. I like to use it as an accent when cooking fish or meat.

Serrano chile A narrow, dark green (or sometimes red) fresh chile about 2 inches long. They are usually spicier than jalapeños, though their heat level varies.

Sesame oil The recipes in this book call for toasted, or Asian, sesame oil, which has an aromatic scent and nutty flavor.

Shallots Similar to an onion in flavor, but less sharp, which makes them suitable for use in salad dressings. White or yellow onions are a fine substitute in cooking, though they take several minutes longer to soften.

Shiitake A specialty mushroom with a nuanced, meaty flavor sold fresh and dried. It has a brown cap and a thin, white, inedible stem.

Spring onions Immature onions with a mild flavor and juicy texture, sold at farmers' markets and specialty stores in spring. They resemble leeks with a white or red rounded end.

Tahini A paste made of ground sesame seeds and sesame oil used in Middle Eastern salads and dips such as hummus.

Thai curry paste A mix of ground chiles, aromatics, and other seasonings sold fresh and in jars as a base for Thai curry dishes. The heat level varies, so use with care.

Recipes by Cuisine

KID-FRIENDLY

LATIN AND LATIN-INSPIRED

LIGHT

Main courses with fewer than 350 calories and 15 grams of fat per serving

Index

Index

Acknowledgments

The best thing about working at a newspaper is the group effort that goes into each project. My deepest thanks go to *The San Francisco Chronicle*, led by editor Phil Bronstein. I am indebted to my editors in the Food section, Michael Bauer and Miriam Morgan, who first created "The Working Cook" column and have always provided incredible support. Special thanks to Narda Zacchino for being such a generous and meticulous editor, and to Dorothy Yule for her beautiful design. Craig Lee's food photography is as gorgeous as ever. And thanks to the rest of *The Chronicle* team that put together this book: Jennifer Asche, Nanette Bisher, Kathleen Hennessy, Ann Hill, Dickson Louie and Jennifer Thelen.

Others who contributed their knowledge, style and hard work to this project were freelance copy editor Sharron Wood and food stylist Jen Straus, who was assisted by Max La Rivière-Hedrick. Thanks also to indexer Ken DellaPenta.

At Sterling Publishing Co., I would like to thank Charles Nurnberg, Andrew Martin, Jason Prince, Leigh Ann Ambrosi, Rick Willett, Adria Dougherty, and Kelly Galvin.

The inspirations and ideas of *The Chronicle's* Food and Wine staff are an integral part of this book. Thanks especially to recipe editor Fran Irwin; to Amanda Berne, Sonia Fuentes, Amanda Gold and Carol Ness, who tested many of the recipes; and to former staffers Robin Davis, Lesli Neilson and Kim Severson.

The friends who tried out the recipes in their homes — Michelle Arkin, Alicia Connor, Nora Dolan, Carrie Emison, Robert Landon, Michele Posner, and Sharron Wood — brought an invaluable perspective.

Most of all, I am grateful for the support and encouragement of my family, especially Jane and Michael Duggan, Dorothy and Arthur Sprague, and, finally, Eric and Dahlia, who were always there when dinner was ready.

Credits

All photography is by *San Francisco Chronicle* staff photographers.

Craig Lee shot all the photos in this book except:

Page 16: photo of basil by Paul Chinn
Page 17: photo of bay leaves by Chris Stewart
        photo of saffron by Lacy Atkins
        photo of garlic by Chris Hardy
        photo of olive oil by Mike Kepka
Page 19: photo of mandoline by Jerry Telfer